Biology

Multiple Choice and Matching

Writing team
James Torrance
James Fullarton
Clare Marsh
James Simms
Caroline Stevenson

Diagrams by
James Torrance

HODDER GIBSON
AN HACHETTE UK COMPANY

Cover photo: The crab has been temporarily submerged by a wave from the incoming tide. It is expelling excess sea water from its gills as two jets. Photo courtesy of James Torrance.

The Publishers would like to thank the following for permission to reproduce copyright material:

Photo credits

p.1 (background) and Unit 1 running head image © Guido Vrola – Fotolia, (insets) © James Torrance; p.59 (background) and Unit 2 running head image © lvcandy – Fotolia, (insets) © James Torrance; p.103 (background) and Unit 3 running head image © Franck Boston – Fotolia, (inset left) © Danicek – Fotolia, (inset centre) © Hfox – Fotolia, (inset right) © James Torrance.

Every effort has been made to trace all copyright holders, but if any have been inadvertently overlooked the Publishers will be pleased to make the necessary arrangements at the first opportunity.

Although every effort has been made to ensure that website addresses are correct at time of going to press, Hodder Gibson cannot be held responsible for the content of any website mentioned in this book. It is sometimes possible to find a relocated web page by typing in the address of the home page for a website in the URL window of your browser.

Hachette UK's policy is to use papers that are natural, renewable and recyclable products and made from wood grown in sustainable forests. The logging and manufacturing processes are expected to conform to the environmental regulations of the country of origin.

Orders: please contact Bookpoint Ltd, 130 Park Drive, Milton Park, Abingdon, Oxon OX14 4SE. Telephone: (44) 01235 827720. Fax: (44) 01235 400454. Lines are open 9.00–5.00, Monday to Saturday, with a 24-hour message answering service. Visit our website at www.hoddereducation.co.uk. Hodder Gibson can be contacted direct on: Tel: 0141 848 1609; Fax: 0141 889 6315; email: hoddergibson@hodder.co.uk

Illustrations by James Torrance

Typeset in Minion Regular 11/14 pt by Integra Software Services Pvt. Ltd., Pondicherry, India

Printed in Slovenia

A catalogue record for this title is available from the British Library

Contents

Preface

This book has been written specifically to complement the textbook *National 5 Biology*. It is intended to act as a valuable resource to pupils and teachers by providing a set of matching exercises and a comprehensive bank of multiple choice questions, the content of which adheres closely to the SQA syllabus for National 5 Biology.

Each test corresponds to a key area of the syllabus and to a chapter in the text book. The matching exercises enable pupils to gradually construct a glossary of terms essential to the course. The multiple choice components contain a variety of types of item, many testing *knowledge and understanding*, some testing *problem-solving skills* and others testing *practical abilities*. These allow pupils to practise extensively in preparation for the examination. The book concludes with three 20-item specimen examinations in the style of the multiple choice section of the externally assessed N5 examination paper.

Unit 1

Cell Biology

1 Cell structure

Matching test

Match the terms in list X with their descriptions in list Y.

list X
1) cell membrane
2) cell wall
3) central vacuole
4) chloroplast
5) cytoplasm
6) micrometre
7) millimetre
8) mitochondrion
9) nucleus
10) organelle
11) plasmid
12) ribosome

list Y
a) unit of length that is one thousandth of a metre
b) unit of length that is one thousandth of a millimetre
c) general term for a functionally discrete, subcellular structure normally surrounded by a membrane
d) tiny circular structure in a bacterium involved in the transfer of genes from one cell to another
e) tiny structure in a cell's cytoplasm that lacks a membrane and is the site of protein synthesis
f) large, normally spherical structure that contains chromosomes and controls the cell's activities
g) liquid-filled, sac-like structure in a plant cell that regulates the water content of the cell and stores solutes
h) fluid or jelly-like 'background' material in which many biochemical reactions occur in all cells
i) thin layer surrounding the cytoplasm that controls the movement of substances into and out of the cell
j) discus-shaped organelle containing green chlorophyll to trap light energy for photosynthesis
k) sausage-shaped organelle responsible for aerobic respiration
l) mesh of cellulose fibres that surrounds and supports a plant cell

Multiple choice test

Choose the ONE correct answer to each of the following multiple choice questions.

Questions 1, 2 and 3 refer to Figure 1.1 of a yeast cell.

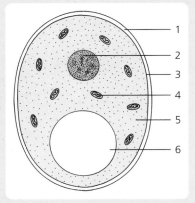

Figure 1.1

Questions 1 and 2 refer to the following possible answers.
    A mitochondrion   **B** cytoplasm   **C** nucleus   **D** vacuole

1 What name is given to structure 2?
2 Identify structure 4.
3 Which parts of this yeast cell would ALL be found in a cheek epithelial cell from a person's mouth?
    A 1, 2 and 3   **B** 2, 3 and 4   **C** 1, 5 and 6   **D** 2, 3 and 6

4   Table 1.1 contains triplets of cell features. Which row gives features that are ALL found in a bacterial cell?

	triplet of cell features		
A	plasmids	cell wall	chloroplasts
B	circular chromosome	mitochondria	plasmids
C	circular chromosome	cell wall	plasmids
D	nucleus	circular chromosome	cell wall

Table 1.1

Questions 5, 6, 7, 8, 9 and 10 refer to Figure 1.2 of a leaf cell.

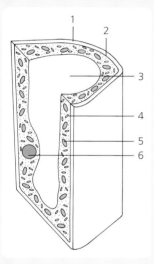

Figure 1.2

5   Which structure is responsible for controlling the cell's activities?
   A 3   **B** 4   **C** 5   **D** 6

6   Which structure would a bacterial cell possess?
   A 2   **B** 3   **C** 4   **D** 5

7   Which structure is composed of cellulose fibres?
   A 1   **B** 2   **C** 3   **D** 6

Questions 8, 9 and 10 refer to the following possible answers.
   A to store water and solutes as cell sap
   B to absorb light energy for photosynthesis
   C to control the passage of substances into the cell
   D to generate energy by aerobic respiration

8   Which answer gives the function of structure 2?

9   Which answer refers to the function of structure 3?

10 Which answer describes the function carried out by structure 5?

Questions 11 and 12 refer to the microscope shown in Figure 1.3.

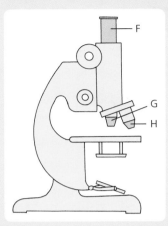

Figure 1.3

11 The nosepiece should be rotated slightly to click the objective lens into place if the image is
    A   out of focus.
    B   poorly illuminated.
    C   half light and half dark.
    D   surrounded by air bubbles.
12 If F contains a lens with a magnification of x15 and G and H give a magnification of x10 and x40, respectively, then the levels of magnification possible for this microscope are
    A   x15 and x50   B   x25 and x55   C   x150 and x400   D   x150 and x600

Questions 13 and 14 refer to Figure 1.4. The left side shows the field of view of a microscope when a plastic ruler with its scale in millimetres (mm) was placed on the microscope's stage. The right side shows a sample of cells from a plant tissue viewed using the same microscope at the same magnification.

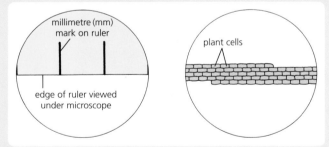

Figure 1.4

13 The diameter of the field of view in micrometres (µm) is
    A   3   B   30   C   300   D   3000
14 The average length of a cell in micrometres (µm) is
    A   0.2   B   2   C   20   D   200

15 Figure 1.5 shows a type of *Paramecium*, a unicellular animal that lives in pond water.

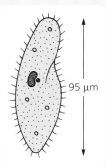

95 μm

Figure 1.5

Which of the following expresses the length of this specimen as a decimal fraction of a millimetre (mm)?

A   0.95   B   0.095   C   0.0095   D   0.00095

2 Transport across cell membranes

Matching test
Match the terms in list X with their descriptions in list Y.

list X
1) active
2) concentration gradient
3) contractile vacuole
4) diffusion
5) osmosis
6) passive
7) phospholipid
8) plasmolysed
9) protein
10) selectively permeable
11) sodium/potassium pump
12) turgid

list Y
a) type of molecule, many of which make up a double layer in a cell membrane
b) type of molecule, many of which are arranged as a patchy mosaic in the cell membrane
c) describing a membrane that allows rapid movement through it of small molecules (such as water) but not large molecules
d) protein carrier molecule in a cell membrane that actively transports one type of ion into the cell and another type out
e) structure used by a unicellular animal to remove excess water gained by osmosis
f) the difference in concentration that exists between two regions resulting in diffusion of molecules (or ions)
g) the process involving the movement of molecules (or ions) from a region of higher concentration to a region of lower concentration
h) term describing the transport of molecules (or ions) down a concentration gradient where no energy is required
i) term describing the transport of molecules (or ions) against a concentration gradient where energy is required
j) term describing a plant cell (or tissue) swollen with water taken in by osmosis
k) term describing a plant cell whose contents have shrunk and pulled away from the cell wall as a result of excessive water loss by osmosis
l) net movement of water molecules from a higher water concentration to a lower water concentration through a selectively permeable membrane

Multiple choice test
Choose the ONE correct answer to each of the following multiple choice questions.

1 Figure 2.1 shows a simplified version of the structure of a cell membrane.

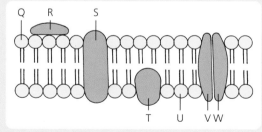

Figure 2.1

Which pair of structures lettered in the diagram are correctly identified in Table 2.1?

	protein	phospholipid
A	Q	T
B	R	U
C	S	V
D	U	W

Table 2.1

Questions 2 and 3 refer to Table 2.2.

	In which direction do the molecules (or ions) move?	Do the molecules (or ions) move down or against a concentration gradient?
A	high to low concentration	against
B	low to high concentration	down
C	high to low concentration	down
D	low to high concentration	against

Table 2.2

2 Which row refers to the process of diffusion?
3 Which row refers to the process of active transport?
4 Which part of Figure 2.2 correctly depicts diffusion of oxygen and CO_2 during gas exchange between an air sac and a blood capillary in the mammalian lung?

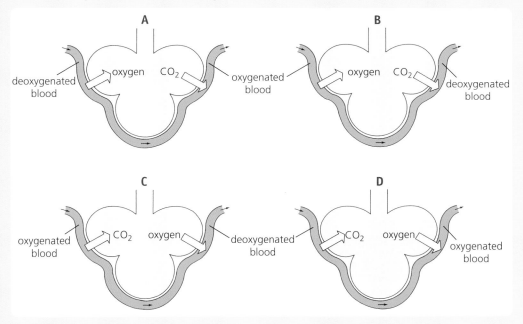

Figure 2.2

5 Figure 2.3 shows ways in which molecules may move into and out of a green plant cell respiring in darkness. Which of these could be diffusion of carbon dioxide molecules?

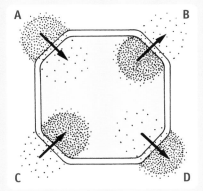

Figure 2.3

6 Osmosis can be defined as the net flow of water molecules through a selectively permeable membrane from a region of
   A high water concentration to a region of lower water concentration.
   B high solute concentration to a region of lower solute concentration.
   C low water concentration to a region of higher water concentration.
   D low solute concentration to a region of lower solute concentration.

7 Which of the following sucrose solutions has the highest water concentration?
   A 1.1 molar   B 0.8 molar   C 0.5 molar   D 0.1 molar

Questions 8 and 9 refer to Figure 2.4. It shows the results of an experiment where turnip cylinders, initially measuring 5 cm in length, were immersed in three different liquids for 24 hours. The test tubes were kept in a thermostatically controlled water bath during this time.

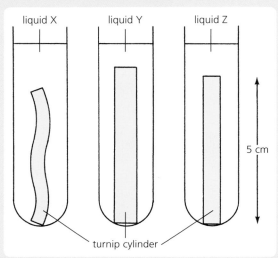

Figure 2.4

8 Which row in Table 2.3 correctly identifies liquids X, Y and Z?

	bathing liquid		
	X	Y	Z
A	1 molar sucrose	0.3 molar sucrose	pure water
B	0.3 molar sucrose	pure water	1 molar sucrose
C	0.3 molar sucrose	1 molar sucrose	pure water
D	1 molar sucrose	pure water	0.3 molar sucrose

Table 2.3

9 The factor that was varied in this experiment was the
   A temperature of bathing liquid.
   B length of turnip cylinder.
   C concentration of sucrose solution.
   D diameter of turnip cylinder.

10 Figure 2.5 shows a visking tubing cell model set up to investigate the process of osmosis.

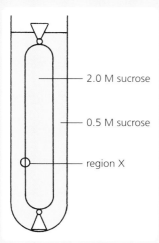

Figure 2.5

Which part of Figure 2.6 most accurately represents region X in Figure 2.5 at the molecular level?

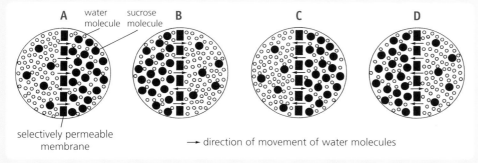

Figure 2.6

Questions 11, 12, 13 and 14 refer to the following information.

In an experiment, groups of 100 potato discs were blotted dry and weighed. Each group was then immersed in one of a series of sucrose solutions. After 4 hours, each group was blotted and reweighed. The results are shown in Table 2.4.

molar concentration of sucrose solution (M)	initial mass of 100 potato discs (g)	final mass of 100 potato discs (g)	gain (+) or loss (–) in mass of 100 potato discs (g)	% gain (+) or loss (–) in mass of 100 potato discs
0.1	20.00	21.00	+1.00	+5.00
0.2	20.00	20.40	+0.40	+2.00
0.3	20.00	19.80	−0.20	−1.00
0.4	22.00	21.12	−0.88	−4.00
0.5	21.00	19.53	−1.47	box X

Table 2.4

11 Which of the graphs shown in Figure 2.7 represents the results for the first four solutions?

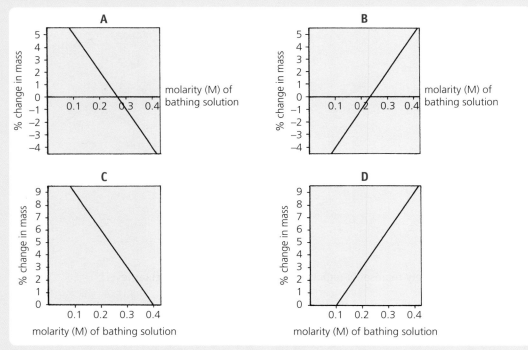

Figure 2.7

12 Which molarity of sucrose solution has a water concentration closest to that of potato cell sap?
  A 0.1 M   **B** 0.2 M   **C** 0.3 M   **D** 0.4 M

13 Box X in Table 2.4 should read
  A 7.00   **B** 7.50   **C** −7.00   **D** −7.50

14 In this experiment it is necessary to convert the results to PERCENTAGE gain or loss in mass in order to
  A compensate for the fact that 100 discs were used.
  B eliminate the need to repeat the experiment.
  C avoid the need to pool results.
  D standardise the results.

15 Figure 2.8 shows a normal red blood cell immersed in 0.85% salt solution.

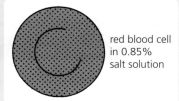
red blood cell in 0.85% salt solution

Figure 2.8

Which part of Figure 2.9 shows the appearance of a red blood cell immersed in 2% salt solution?

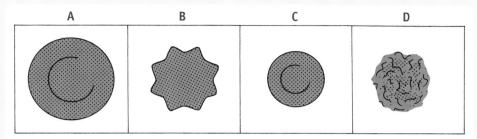

Figure 2.9

16 A *stentor* is a unicellular animal which lives in pond water equal in water concentration to 0.1% salt solution. It uses its two contractile vacuoles to remove excess water from its body.

If a *stentor* was moved from its normal environment to pure water, its contractile vacuoles would

A   stop working until normal conditions returned.
B   continue to work at their normal rate.
C   increase their rate of emptying.
D   decrease their rate of emptying.

Questions 17, 18 and 19 refer to Figure 2.10 which shows plant cells that have been immersed in solutions of different water concentration.

 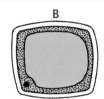

Figure 2.10

17 In which cell has plasmolysis just begun?
18 Which cell is immersed in the most concentrated sugar solution?
19 Which cell is turgid?

Questions 20 and 21 refer to the graph in Figure 2.11. It shows a graph of the results from an experiment where each of four potato cylinders was immersed in a different chemical for a standard length of time and then placed in water for the same length of time.

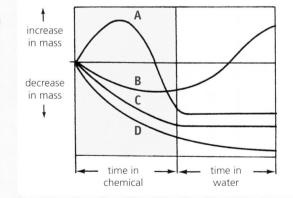

key
A = cylinder A in chemical A
B = cylinder B in chemical B
C = cylinder C in chemical C
D = cylinder D in chemical D

20 Which chemical was NOT toxic (poisonous) to the selectively permeable membranes of the potato cells?

21 Deplasmolysis is the opposite process from plasmolysis. In which cylinder did deplasmolysis take place?

Figure 2.11

Questions 22, 23 and 24 refer to Figure 2.12. It shows the transport of two types of ion through the membrane of an animal cell. The carrier molecule is called the sodium/potassium pump because it exchanges one type of ion for the other.

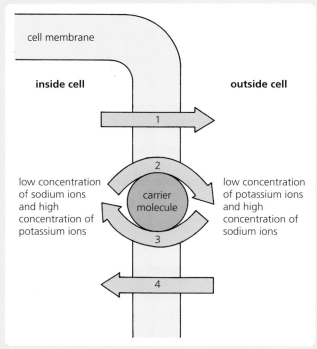

inside cell

outside cell

cell membrane

low concentration of sodium ions and high concentration of potassium ions

carrier molecule

low concentration of potassium ions and high concentration of sodium ions

Figure 2.12

22 Diffusion of potassium ions occurs at arrow
   A 1   B 2   C 3   D 4

23 Active transport of sodium ions occurs at arrow
   A 1   B 2   C 3   D 4

24 Cyanide is a respiratory poison. Application of cyanide to the cell shown would affect and bring to a halt the processes indicated by arrows
   A 1 and 4 only.
   B 3 and 4 only.
   C 2 and 3 only.
   D 1, 2, 3 and 4.

25 Table 2.5 refers to the concentrations of certain chemical ions in the cells of a species of a simple water plant and in the surrounding pond water.

ion	concentration of ion in cell sap (units)	concentration of ion in pond water (units)	accumulation ratio
calcium (Ca^{2+})	15.6	1.3	12:1
chloride (Cl^-)	104.0	1.0	104:1
magnesium (Mg^{2+})	17.4	box X	6:1
sodium (Na^+)	67.2	1.2	box Y

Table 2.5

Which row in Table 2.6 gives the correct answers to boxes X and Y in Table 2.5?

	box X	box Y
A	2.9	56:1
B	2.9	81:1
C	104.4	56:1
D	104.4	81:1

Table 2.6

Matching test
Match the terms in list X with their descriptions in list Y.

list X
1) aseptic technique
2) cell culture
3) chromatid
4) chromosome
5) chromosome complement
6) contaminant
7) diploid
8) equator
9) fermenter
10) growth medium
11) haploid
12) inoculation
13) mitosis
14) replication
15) spindle

list Y
a) central region of the spindle where chromosomes (each attached to a spindle fibre) are found immediately prior to nuclear division
b) web-like structure made of cytoplasmic fibres to which chromosomes become attached
c) term describing a body cell which contains two matching sets of chromosomes
d) term describing a sex cell which contains a single set of chromosomes
e) growth of a population of one type of cell in or on suitable growth medium
f) precaution taken to try to create sterile conditions during an investigation
g) nutrient agar or broth containing an energy source and nutrients needed by the microorganism to build new cells
h) container in which a fermentation process is brought about by a microorganism
i) reproduction of a chromosome into two exact copies of itself called chromatids
j) transfer of a sample of microorganisms from a pure culture to a sterile container of growth medium
k) stray microbe or other unwanted material that has gained access to a cell culture's growth medium
l) process by which a cell's nucleus divides into two identical nuclei each with the same number of chromosomes as the original nucleus
m) one of two identical thread-like structures formed by the replication of a chromosome
n) thread-like structure present in the nucleus that replicates forming two identical chromatids
o) definite and characteristic number of chromosomes present in each cell of a species

➡

Multiple choice test

Choose the ONE correct answer to each of the following multiple choice questions.

1 Figure 3.1 shows stages that occur during mitosis and cell division.

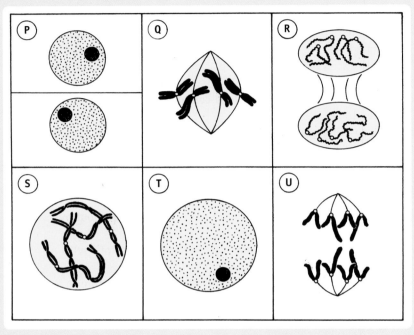

Figure 3.1

The sequence in which these stages occur is

A T, S, Q, R, U, P.   **B** T, Q, S, R, U, P.   **C** T, S, Q, U, R, P.   **D** T, Q, S, U, R, P.

2 Figure 3.2 shows the nucleus of a cell undergoing mitosis.

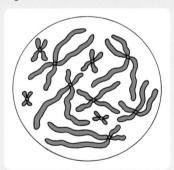

Figure 3.2

Which row in Table 3.1 is correct?

	number of pairs of chromosomes present	number of chromatids present	number of chromosomes that each daughter cell will receive following mitosis
A	5	20	10
B	5	40	5
C	10	20	10
D	10	40	5

Table 3.1

3 Table 3.2 gives the times taken by stages that occur before and during mitosis and cell division in a type of cell in maize plants.

order of stages	symbol representing stage	description of stage	time taken by stage (h)
1	G_1	cell growth	13
2	S	production of chromatids	4
3	G_2	further cell growth	5
4	M	mitosis	3

Table 3.2

Which pie chart in Figure 3.3 correctly represents the data in Table 3.2?

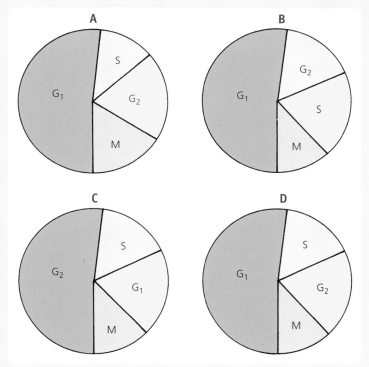

Figure 3.3

4 Figure 3.4 shows one of the stages that occurs during mitosis.

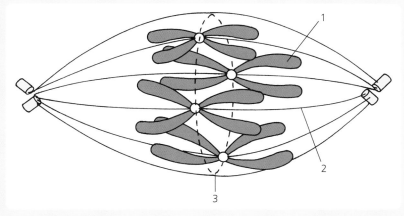

Figure 3.4

Which row in Table 3.3 correctly identifies structures 1, 2 and 3?

	1	2	3
A	chromatid	spindle fibre	equator
B	spindle fibre	chromatid	equator
C	equator	spindle fibre	chromatid
D	chromatid	equator	spindle fibre

Table 3.3

Questions 5 and 6 refer to Table 3.4, which shows the results from an investigation into the effect of temperature on the time taken by a type of human cell to complete the stages involved in nuclear and cell division.

temperature (°C)	time taken by stage of nuclear and cell division (h)			
	stage M	stage G_1	stage S	stage G_2
33	13.0	26.0	22.4	12.2
36	1.5	13.0	7.4	3.9
38	0.8	7.5	7.2	3.3

Table 3.4

5 How long in minutes did stage M take at 38°C?
   A 8   B 48   C 80   D 480
6 From the data it can be concluded that an increase in temperature brings about
   A a decrease in length of time taken by each stage.
   B an increase in length of time taken by each stage.
   C no significant change in length of time taken by each stage.
   D erratic changes in length of time taken that fail to show a definite trend.
7 Each normal body cell in a chimpanzee contains 48 chromosomes. In Figure 3.5, the numbers refer to the chromosomes present in each body cell. Which part of the diagram correctly represents two successive cycles of mitosis and cell division?

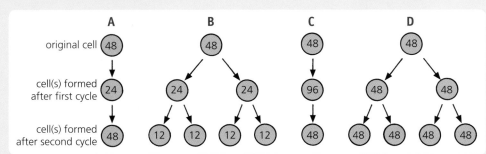

Figure 3.5

8   A human sperm contains 23 chromosomes, an onion root tip cell contains 16 chromosomes and a fruit fly egg contains 4 chromosomes. Which row in Table 3.5 is correct?

	number of chromosomes in a diploid cell of the organism		
	human	onion	fruit fly
A	23	16	4
B	23	32	4
C	46	16	8
D	46	32	8

Table 3.5

Questions 9 and 10 refer to the graph in Figure 3.6. It shows the results of an investigation into cell division in human skin cells.

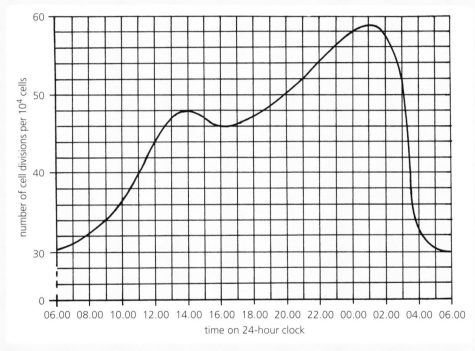

Figure 3.6

9   The increase in the number of cell divisions per 10^4 cells that occurred between 16.00 and midnight was
     A   6   B   8   C   12   D   13

10 For how many hours did the number of cell divisions remain below 38 per 10^4 cells?
     A   3.5   B   7   C   8   D   17

11 Figure 3.7 shows the early stages in the development of a type of animal from a fertilised egg to a multicellular embryo.

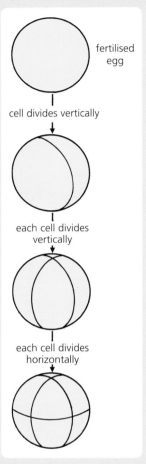

fertilised egg

cell divides vertically

each cell divides vertically

each cell divides horizontally

Figure 3.7

How many cells will be present in the embryo after three further rounds of cell division?

A 32　　　　　B 64　　　　　C 128　　　　　D 256

Questions 12 and 13 refer to the graph in Figure 3.8. It shows the change in the number of yeast cells cultured in a solution of glucose for 24 hours.

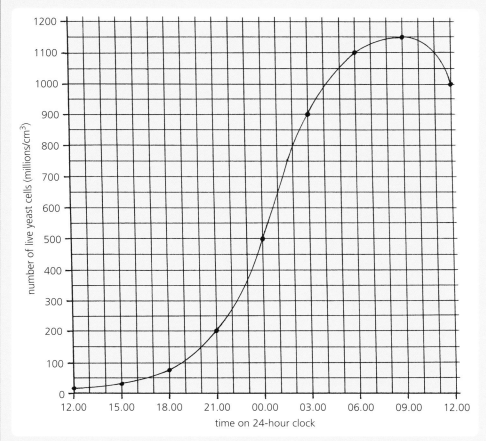

Figure 3.8

12 Between which times did the number of yeast cells show the greatest increase?

  A 18.00 and 21.00   **B** 21.00 and 00.00   **C** 00.00 and 03.00   **D** 03.00 and 06.00

13 How many hours did it take the culture to increase in number from 150 million cells per cm^3 to seven times this number?

  A 7   **B** 8   **C** 9   **D** 10

14 The graph in Figure 3.9 shows the rate of increase in height of boys and girls between the ages of 6 months and 18 years (based on data from a large population).

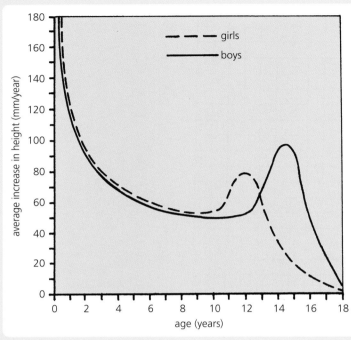

Figure 3.9

On average the girls showed an annual gain in height of 80 mm at ages

A 3 and 12   B 3 and 13   C 3 and 15   D 13 and 15

15 The graph in Figure 3.10 charts the growth in length of a human fetus before birth.

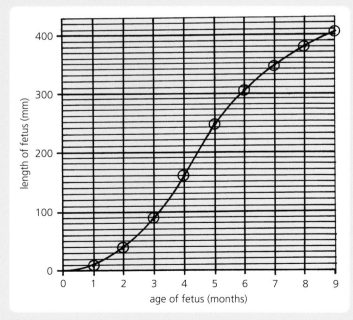

Figure 3.10

What was the average rate of growth of the fetus in mm/month during the final 4 months of pregnancy?

A 25   B 40   C 160   D 405

16 Figure 3.11 shows a simple version of an industrial fermenter being used to culture bacteria. Which tube would be used for the release of waste gases?

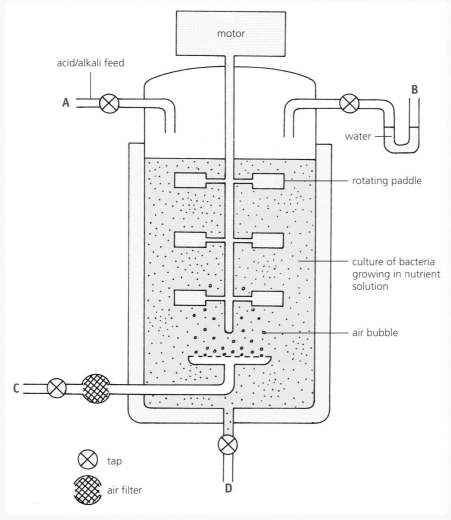

Figure 3.11

17 Figure 3.12 shows four steps carried out to grow a culture of yeast cells on nutrient agar.

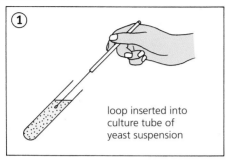

① loop inserted into culture tube of yeast suspension

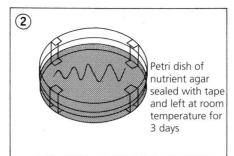

② Petri dish of nutrient agar sealed with tape and left at room temperature for 3 days

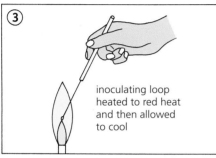

③ inoculating loop heated to red heat and then allowed to cool

④ lid of Petri dish raised and sterile nutrient agar streaked gently in zig-zag line using loop

Figure 3.12

What is the correct order of the four steps?

A 1, 3, 2, 4.   B 1, 3, 4, 2.   C 3, 1, 2, 4.   D 3, 1, 4, 2.

18 Which part of Figure 3.13 shows a simple fermenter correctly set up and ready for use?

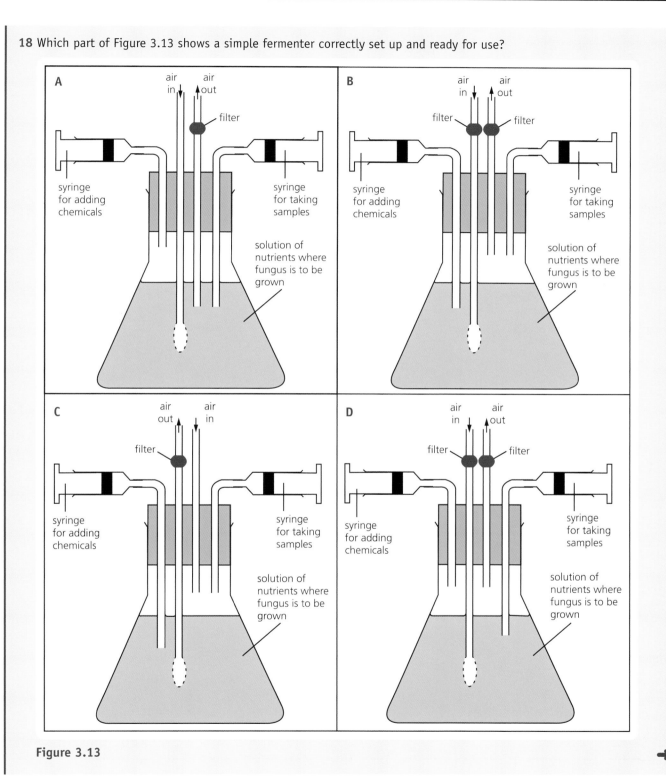

Figure 3.13

Questions 19 and 20 refer to Figure 3.14. It shows Petri dishes set up to investigate the effect of two types of nutrient medium (X and Y) on bacterial growth under different conditions of pH and temperature.

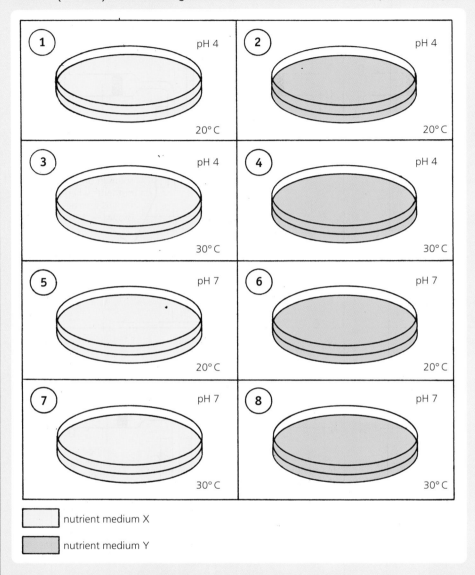

nutrient medium X

nutrient medium Y

Figure 3.14

19 Which two dishes should be compared to find out the effect of pH at 30°C using nutrient medium X?

| A 3 and 7 | B 3 and 4 | C 5 and 7 | D 4 and 8 |

20 Which of the following comparisons is the only one that would allow a valid conclusion to be drawn from the results?

| A 1 and 7 | B 5 and 6 | C 3 and 5 | D 6 and 7 |

4 DNA and the production of proteins

Matching test
Match the terms in list X with their descriptions in list Y.

list X
1) adenine (A)
2) amino acid
3) base
4) cytosine (C)
5) DNA
6) double helix
7) gene
8) genetic code
9) guanine (G)
10) mRNA
11) ribosome
12) thymine (T)

list Y
a) sub-cellular structure which is the site of protein synthesis
b) a region of DNA on a chromosome which codes for a protein
c) molecular component of protein
d) general term for molecular component of DNA
e) two-stranded molecule of DNA wound into a spiral
f) molecular language determined by the sequence of bases in a DNA chain
g) type of nucleic acid present in chromosomes
h) type of nucleic acid which carries a complementary copy of the genetic code from DNA to a ribosome
i) base present in DNA which is complementary to adenine (A)
j) base present in DNA which is complementary to thymine (T)
k) base present in DNA which is complementary to cytosine (C)
l) base present in DNA which is complementary to guanine (G)

Multiple choice test
Choose the ONE correct answer to each of the following multiple choice questions.

Questions 1, 2 and 3 refer to Figure 4.1. It shows part of a cell's genetic material.

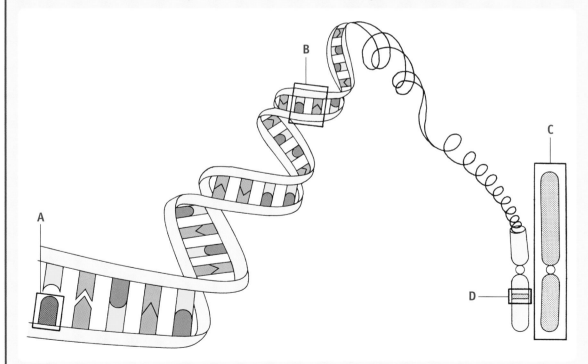

Figure 4.1

1 Which boxed region represents a complete gene?
2 Which boxed region represents a DNA base?
3 Which boxed region represents a chromosome?

4 The information present in a species' DNA takes the form of a molecular language called the
   A genome.   **B** genotype.   **C** gene pool.   **D** genetic code.
5 Which of boxes A–D shown in Figure 4.2 contains the DNA strand that is complementary to the one in box X?

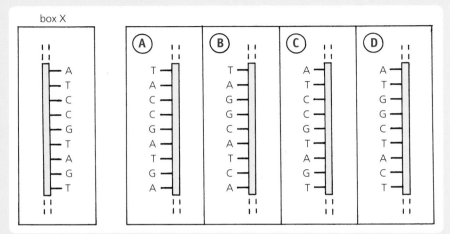

Figure 4.2

6 Which of the following represents one of Chargaff's rules about the bases present in a molecule of DNA?
   A The number of T bases equals the number of C bases.
   B The number of A bases equals the number of G bases.
   C The number of T bases equals the number of A bases.
   D The number of G bases equals the number of T bases.
7 Figure 4.3 shows a small part of a DNA molecule where the four types of base molecule are represented by the letters A, T, G and C.

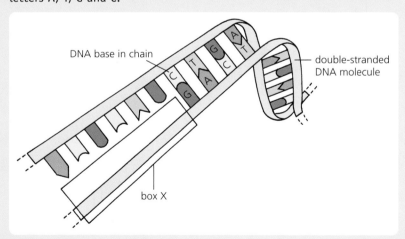

Figure 4.3

Which part of Figure 4.4 below supplies the information missing from box X in Figure 4.3?

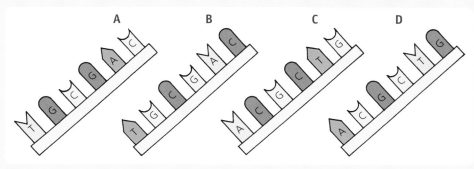

Figure 4.4

8 If a DNA molecule contains 8000 base molecules and 2400 of these are cytosine, then the percentage number of thymine bases present in the molecule is

A 16   B 20   C 24   D 30

9 If a DNA molecule contains 20 000 base molecules of which 22% are adenine, then the number of guanine base molecules present is

A 4400   B 4600   C 5600   D 112 000

10 Figure 4.5 shows two types of eye found amongst fruit flies. The only difference in chromosome structure that exists between the two types of fly is a duplicated section.

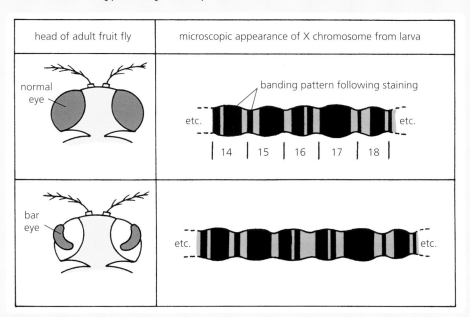

Figure 4.5

On which numbered section of the X chromosome is the gene for the bar eye located?

A 15   B 16   C 17   D 18

11 Each human being inherits 50% of their DNA from each parent. Following extraction and separation of a person's DNA by special techniques, a pattern of bands is formed. This pattern is unique to the person and is called a DNA fingerprint. Figure 4.6 represents DNA fingerprints of seven people.

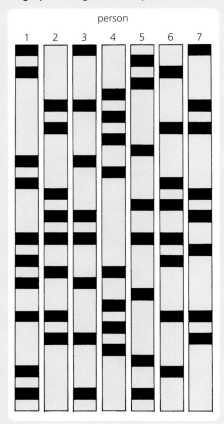

Figure 4.6

Who are the parents of person 1?

A   2 and 4   B   3 and 5   C   5 and 7   D   3 and 6

12 Which row in Table 4.1 correctly identifies blanks 1, 2 and 3 in the following pair of statements?

A molecule of __1__ consists of a __2__ helix held together by base pairs. The base sequence in the nucleic acid determines the order in which __3__ acids become assembled into a protein molecule.

	blank 1	blank 2	blank 3
A	DNA	single-stranded	nucleic
B	mRNA	single-stranded	amino
C	DNA	double-stranded	amino
D	mRNA	double-stranded	nucleic

Table 4.1

13 Figure 4.7 shows the stages involved in the production of a protein.

> (1) A strand of mRNA is produced which is complementary to one of the DNA strands.

> (2) Amino acids are assembled into protein in a sequence determined by the order of the bases on the mRNA.

> (3) A region of the DNA molecule becomes uncoiled and opens up.

> (4) The mRNA molecule passes out of the nucleus into the cytoplasm of the cell.

Figure 4.7

The order in which they occur is

A 1, 3, 2, 4   B 1, 3, 4, 2   C 3, 1, 2, 4   D 3, 1, 4, 2

14 The assembly of a protein molecule from its sub-units takes place in a cell at a

A nucleus.   B ribosome.   C chromosome.   D mitochondrion.

15 Figure 4.8 shows a small part of a strand of mRNA. Table 4.2 gives some code words and the amino acids to which they correspond.

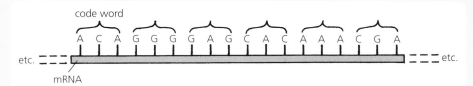

Figure 4.8

code word	amino acid	abbreviation
ACA	threonine	thr
GCG	alanine	ala
CAC	histamine	his
CAG	glutamine	gln
AAA	lysine	lys
GAG	glutamic acid	glu
CGA	arginine	arg
AGC	serine	ser
GGG	glycine	gly

Table 4.2

Which part of Figure 4.9 shows the portion of protein that would be assembled according to the instructions on the mRNA strand in Figure 4.8?

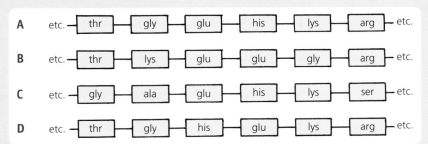

Figure 4.9

5 Proteins and enzymes

Matching test
Match the terms in list X with their descriptions in list Y.

list X
1) amino acid
2) antibody
3) catalyst
4) degradation
5) denatured
6) enzyme
7) hormone
8) optimum
9) product
10) protein
11) receptor
12) specificity
13) substrate
14) synthesis

list Y
a) building-up of large complex molecules from simpler ones by an enzyme-controlled reaction
b) type of organic chemical of which enzymes are composed
c) substance upon which an enzyme acts resulting in the formation of an end product
d) substance which increases the rate of a chemical reaction and remains unaltered
e) protein made by living cells which acts as a biological catalyst
f) enzyme-controlled breakdown of large complex molecules to simpler ones
g) term used to describe the state of an enzyme which has been permanently destroyed
h) molecular component of a protein
i) chemical messenger in an animal's blood which is often made of protein
j) substance formed as a result of an enzyme acting on its substrate
k) type of protein which defends the body against disease-causing microorganisms
l) type of protein which recognises and exactly fits a particular signal molecule
m) term referring to the condition of a factor at which an enzyme works best
n) complementary relationship of molecular structure which allows an enzyme to combine with one substrate only

Multiple choice test
Choose the ONE correct answer to each of the following multiple choice questions.

1 Which row in Table 5.1 correctly identifies the three blanks in the following pair of statements?
A molecule of protein is composed of subunits called ___1___ acids of which there are ___2___ different types. The protein's shape and function are determined by the ___3___ of amino acids that it contains.

	blank 1	blank 2	blank 3
A	fatty	4	number
B	fatty	20	number
C	amino	4	sequence
D	amino	20	sequence

Table 5.1

2 Which row in Table 5.2 is NOT correct?

	type of protein made by human body	function
A	antibiotic	acts as a natural form of defence against disease-causing microorganisms
B	hormone	acts as a chemical messenger to which a target tissue responds
C	receptor	triggers a chemical event when targeted by a signal molecule
D	enzyme	speeds up the rate of a biochemical reaction

Table 5.2

3   Which part of Figure 5.1 correctly represents the role played by a type of receptor protein when one nerve cell sends a signal to another nerve cell?

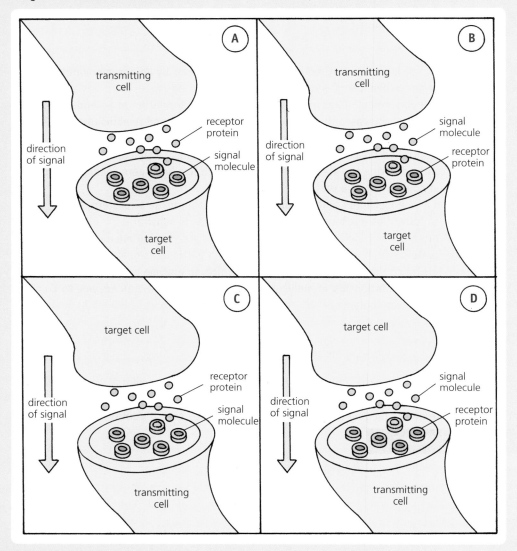

Figure 5.1

4   Each enzyme is a
   A   protein molecule produced by living cells to catalyse a particular biochemical reaction.
   B   living molecule produced by cells to digest food in the alimentary canal.
   C   protein molecule produced by living cells to catalyse a variety of biochemical reactions.
   D   living molecule produced by cells to synthesise complex substances from simpler ones.

5   Figure 5.2 shows four stages that occur during the enzyme-controlled synthesis of a complex molecule.

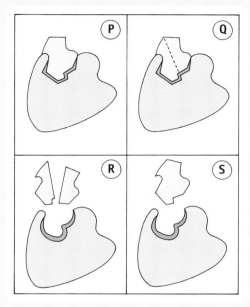

Figure 5.2

What is the correct order of the four stages?

A   Q, S, R, P   B   R, Q, P, S   C   S, P, Q, R   D   R, P, Q, S

Questions 6 and 7 refer to the following possible answers.

A   denatured   B   specific   C   optimum   D   synthetic

6   Which term is used to describe an enzyme that has been destroyed?
7   Which term is used to describe the relationship that exists between a molecule of an enzyme and its substrate?
8   Figure 5.3 shows an experiment set up to investigate the effect of catalase on the breakdown of hydrogen peroxide.

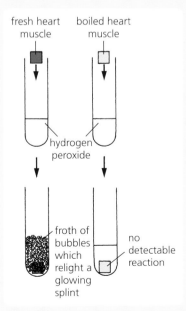

Figure 5.3

Which row in Table 5.3 is correct?

	substrate	end product
A	heart muscle	carbon dioxide
B	hydrogen peroxide	oxygen
C	heart muscle	oxygen
D	hydrogen peroxide	carbon dioxide

Table 5.3

9 In an enzyme experiment set up to investigate the breakdown of protein, 899 μg of amino acids were produced in 2 hours 25 minutes. Expressed in μg/min, the rate of reaction was

    A 6.2   B 7.2   C 10.6   D 130.4

10 A group of students wished to investigate the hypothesis that soaked oat grains and soaked barley grains contain amylase. They set up a Petri dish as shown in Figure 5.4. Each seed was cut in half and the two halves placed cut surface down on the starch agar.

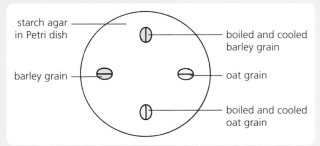

Figure 5.4

After 24 hours the seeds were removed and the dish flooded with iodine solution. Which set of results shown in Figure 5.5 supports the students' hypothesis?

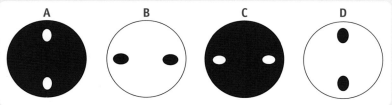

Figure 5.5

11 Figure 5.6 shows an experiment set up to investigate the effect of the enzymes in a snail's gut on starch molecules.

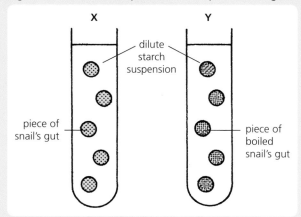

Figure 5.6

Which of the following sets of results would be obtained if the snail's gut contained amylase?

A

	at start		after 2 hours	
	starch test	simple sugar test	starch test	simple sugar test
sample from tube X	+	–	+	–
sample from tube Y	+	–	–	+

B

	at start		after 2 hours	
	starch test	simple sugar test	starch test	simple sugar test
sample from tube X	+	–	–	+
sample from tube Y	–	+	–	+

C

	at start		after 2 hours	
	starch test	simple sugar test	starch test	simple sugar test
sample from tube X	–	+	+	–
sample from tube Y	–	+	–	+

D

	at start		after 2 hours	
	starch test	simple sugar test	starch test	simple sugar test
sample from tube X	+	–	–	+
sample from tube Y	+	–	+	–

Tables 5.4

12 A control is set up to
  A increase the reliability of the results.
  B make the experiment fair in every way.
  C ensure that the results of the experiment are accurate.
  D show that the results are due to the factor being investigated.

Questions 13, 14 and 15 refer to the following information.

Before being used in an experiment, bovine catalase solution, hydrogen peroxide solution and a set of pH buffers were kept in a water bath at 25°C. Uniform volumes of these liquids were then used to investigate the effect of pH on the activity of catalase. The results are shown in Table 5.5.

	pH						
	6	7	8	9	10	11	12
time taken to collect 1 cm³ of oxygen (s)	108	98	57	48	60	86	96

Table 5.5

13 Which of the graphs in Figure 5.7 correctly represents the data in Table 5.5?

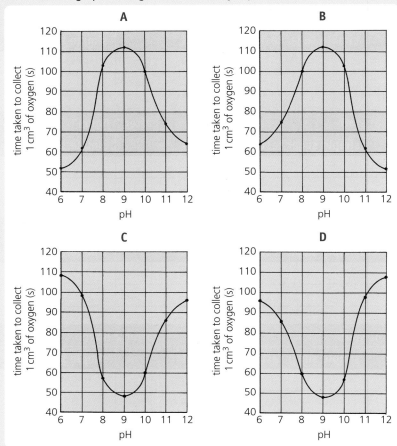

Figure 5.7

14 The enzyme was most active over the pH range
   A 9–11   B 8–10   C 7–9   D 6–8

15 Use of a thermostatically controlled water bath in this experiment is necessary to ensure that
   A   the experiment contains a valid set of controls.
   B   temperature is the only variable factor under investigation.
   C   the results obtained during the experiment are accurate.
   D   the temperature is equal in all tubes at the start of the experiment.

Questions 16, 17, 18, and 19 refer to the following information.

An unusual enzyme has been extracted from a species of bacterium. Table 5.6 shows the percentage of protein that is digested by this enzyme at different temperatures and levels of pH.

		percentage digestion at temperature (°C) of:			
		40	50	60	70
percentage digestion at pH of:	5	12	19	31	2
	7	61	73	88	21
	9	67	85	97	33
	11	16	25	42	3

Table 5.6

16 The optimum pH for the activity of this enzyme is

   A 5   **B** 7   **C** 9   **D** 11

17 The optimum temperature (in °C) for the activity of this enzyme is

   A 40   **B** 50   **C** 60   **D** 70

18 Which of the following would be the MOST likely percentage of protein digested by the enzyme at pH 8 and temperature 55°C?

   A 68   **B** 71   **C** 86   **D** 99

19 By how many times is the percentage of protein digested at 60°C and pH 11 greater than that digested at 40°C and pH 5?

   A 3.5   **B** 35.0   **C** 50.4   **D** 504.0

20 The experiment shown in Figure 5.8 and the results in Table 5.7 refer to an investigation involving the action of the enzyme catalase.

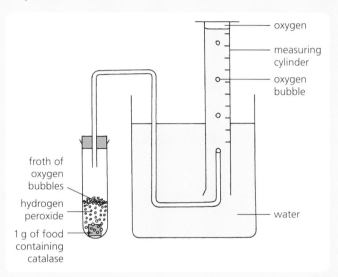

Figure 5.8

trial number	time required to collect 1 cm³ of oxygen (s)		
	carrot	potato	heart muscle
1	133	87	40
2	147	91	42
3	129	89	39
4	151	107	box Q
5	165	96	45
mean	145	box P	42

Table 5.7

Which row in Table 5.8 below gives the correct answers to boxes P and Q in Table 5.7?

	box P	box Q
A	78	42
B	78	44
C	94	42
D	94	44

Table 5.8

Questions 21 and 22 refer to the graph in Figure 5.9. It shows the rate of an enzyme's activity at different temperatures.

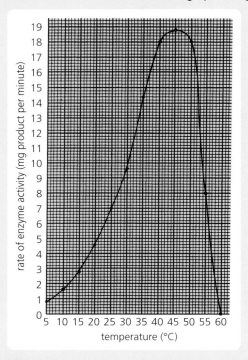

21 The greatest increase in rate of enzyme activity occurred between temperatures

    A 20 and 25°C   **B** 25 and 30°C   **C** 30 and 35°C   **D** 35 and 40°C

22 The greatest change in enzyme activity took place between temperatures

    A 15 and 25°C   **B** 25 and 35°C   **C** 35 and 45°C   **D** 45 and 55°C

Figure 5.9

Questions 23, 24 and 25 refer to the following information.

Trypsin is a protein-digesting enzyme made in the human pancreas. Powdered milk suspension is a source of protein which has a white cloudy appearance. Figure 5.10 shows an investigation into the effect of boiling and into the effect of alkali on the activity of trypsin. This investigation consists of two experiments conducted at the same time.

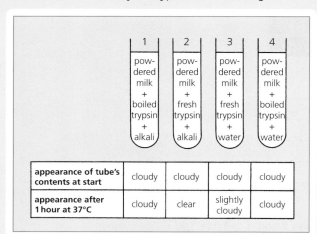

23 Which two tubes should be compared at the end of the experiment to draw a conclusion about the effect of boiling on trypsin's activity?

    A 1 and 2   **B** 2 and 3   **C** 1 and 4   **D** 2 and 4

24 Which two tubes should be compared at the end of the experiment to draw a conclusion about the effect of alkali on trypsin's activity?

    A 1 and 2   **B** 2 and 3   **C** 1 and 4   **D** 3 and 4

25 Which tube is the control in the experiment to investigate the effect of alkali on trypsin?

    A 1   **B** 2   **C** 3   **D** 4

Figure 5.10

6 Genetic engineering

Matching test
Match the terms in list X with their descriptions in list Y.

list X
1) DNA
2) enzymes
3) genetic engineering
4) genetically modified
5) plasmid
6) vector
7) virus

list Y
a) term used to describe an organism after the insertion into it of DNA from another species
b) agent such as a plasmid by means of which a fragment of 'foreign' DNA can be inserted into a host cell
c) genetic material that can be transferred from one species to another by genetic engineering
d) biological catalysts, one type used to cut up DNA, the other to seal DNA into plasmids
e) type of microorganism that can transfer DNA to other species by natural means
f) small circular structure in a bacterium which can be used to transfer genes from one species to another
g) process by which a piece of DNA is removed from one species and inserted into another

Multiple choice test
Choose the ONE correct answer to each of the following multiple choice questions.

Questions 1, 2 and 3 refer to Figure 6.1 which shows the genetic material of a bacterial cell.

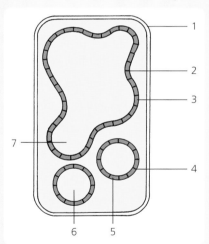

Figure 6.1

1 Which structure is the chromosome?
   A 1   B 2   C 4   D 6
2 Which structure is a plasmid?
   A 2   B 3   C 4   D 7
3 Which structures are BOTH genes?
   A 2 and 3   B 3 and 4   C 3 and 5   D 5 and 6

Questions 4, 5 and 6 refer to the following list of procedural steps employed during genetic engineering.
   1 genetically modified host cell allowed to multiply
   2 required DNA fragment cut out of appropriate chromosome
   3 duplicate plasmids formed which express a 'foreign' gene
   4 plasmid extracted from bacterium and opened up
   5 altered plasmid inserted into bacterial host cell
   6 DNA fragment sealed into plasmid

4 The correct order in which these steps would be carried out is
   A 2, 4, 6, 5, 1, 3   **B** 2, 4, 5, 6, 3, 1   **C** 4, 6, 2, 5, 3, 1   **D** 4, 6, 2, 5, 1, 3
5 A special enzyme that acts as biochemical 'scissors' would be used during the steps
   A 2 and 4   **B** 2 and 6   **C** 4 and 5   **D** 4 and 6
6 A special enzyme that acts as biochemical 'glue' would be used at stage
   A 2   **B** 4   **C** 5   **D** 6
7 Figure 6.2 shows two cells from different species of bacteria about to undergo a natural exchange of plasmids.

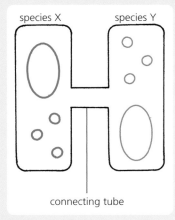

Figure 6.2

Which part of Figure 6.3 shows the outcome of the exchange?

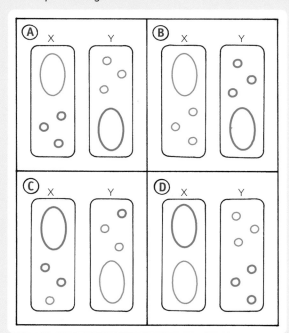

Figure 6.3

8 Which of the statements in the following list correctly refer to genetic engineering?
   1 The genotype of the organism produced becomes altered.
   2 The new variety can make a substance previously only made by a different species.
   3 The process involves working with many generations of the organism over a very long period of time.
   4 The gene for a useful characteristic is transferred from one species to another.
      A 1, 2 and 4   **B** 1, 3 and 4   **C** 2, 3 and 4   **D** 1, 2, 3 and 4

9 Figure 6.4 shows two preparatory stages carried out during the process of genetic engineering.

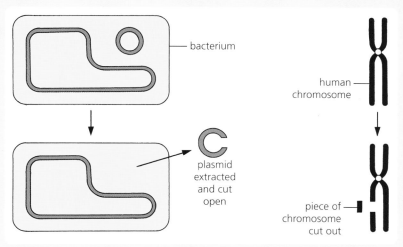

Figure 6.4

Which part of Figure 6.5 shows a later stage in the process?

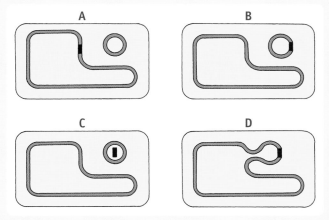

Figure 6.5

10 An example of a transgenic multicellular organism is a
   A bacterium in the soil that invades wounded plant tissue.
   B yeast cell engineered to make lager with a high alcohol content.
   C person who would suffer diabetes without a supply of insulin.
   D crop plant into which a useful gene has been successfully inserted.

Questions 11 and 12 refer to the following information.

Ethylene is a growth substance that promotes the ripening of fruit. Genetic engineers have developed a variety of tomato that makes very little ethylene and takes longer than normal to ripen. The graph in Figure 6.6 shows the results from one of their experiments.

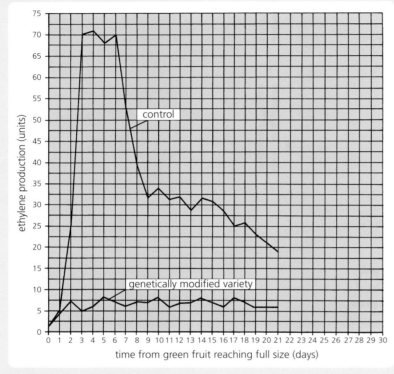

Figure 6.6

11 By how many times was the production of ethylene by the control greater than that by the genetically modified (GM) variety at day 3?

  A 14   **B** 23   **C** 65   **D** 67

12 If the trends in the graph continue, on which day will ethylene production be equal in the two varieties of tomato?

  A 26   **B** 27   **C** 28   **D** 29

Questions 13 and 14 refer to Table 6.1 and to the possible answers that follow it.

genetically modified crop plant	role of inserted gene	beneficial effect
maize	box X	leaves able to resist attack by beetles
soya	production of a chemical that gives resistance to weedkiller	crop survives but weeds die when weedkiller is applied
strawberry	box Y	fruit is protected against damage by frost
tomato	blockage of production of chemical that promotes ripening	shelf life of fruit is extended

Table 6.1

  A production of chemical that promotes ripening
  B production of chemical that can be converted in the human body to vitamin A
  C production of chemical that acts as a natural antifreeze
  D production of chemical that works as a natural insecticide

13 Which answer should have been used to complete box X?

14 Which answer should have been used to complete box Y?

15 The graph in Figure 6.7 shows the number of acres of farmland planted with a type of genetically modified (GM) cotton in a region of the USA.

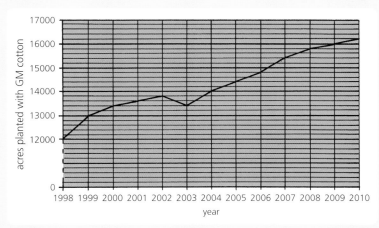

Figure 6.7

What is the percentage increase in number of acres planted with this crop between the years 1998 and 2010?

A   34.1   B   35.0   C   35.8   D   36.7

7 Respiration

Matching test

Match the terms in list X with their descriptions in list Y.

list X
1) aerobic
2) ATP
3) cytoplasm
4) ethanol
5) fermentation
6) glucose
7) kilojoule
8) lactic acid
9) mitochondrion
10) oxygen
11) oxygen debt
12) pyruvate
13) respirometer

list Y
a) chemical formed from the splitting of a molecule of glucose during the first stage of respiration
b) state that develops in muscle tissue during fermentation and is repaid during a rest period
c) unit used to measure energy
d) piece of equipment designed to measure rate of respiration
e) chemical element needed for aerobic respiration
f) chemical formed during fermentation in animal cells
g) chemical formed during fermentation in plant cells
h) a cellular structure within which aerobic respiration is completed in the presence of oxygen
i) type of respiration that occurs in the absence of oxygen and produces a small quantity of energy
j) type of respiration that occurs in the presence of oxygen and produces a large quantity of energy
k) region of the cell where the first stage of respiration occurs
l) high energy compound synthesised using energy from the respiratory breakdown of glucose
m) type of sugar that acts as a source of energy in living cells

Multiple choice test

Choose the ONE correct answer to each of the following multiple choice questions.

1 Which of the following are BOTH materials used in the process of aerobic respiration?
   A glucose and carbon dioxide
   B carbon dioxide and water
   C water and oxygen
   D oxygen and glucose

2 The energy in kilojoules (kJ) released by burning food can be calculated by using the formula $\dfrac{4.2\ MT}{1000}$ where M = mass of water (g) and T = rise in temperature (°C).

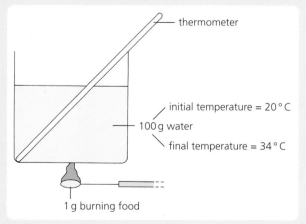

thermometer

initial temperature = 20 °C

100 g water

final temperature = 34 °C

1 g burning food

Figure 7.1

Which of the following gives the number of kilojoules of energy released by the food shown in Figure 7.1?
   A 0.58   **B** 1.42   **C** 5.88   **D** 14.28

Questions 3 and 4 refer to the following information.

4.2 kJ is the quantity of energy required to raise the temperature of 1000 g of water by 1°C. The results in Table 7.1 were obtained by burning 1 g of each food.

food	number of kilojoules (kJ) released on burning 1 g of food
peach	1.5
parsnip	2.1
sweetcorn	4.2
trifle	8.4

Table 7.1

3   When burned, 1 g of one of the foods in the table was found to raise the temperature of 1000 g of water by 0.5°C. Identify the food.

    A   peach   B   parsnip   C   sweetcorn   D   trifle

4   How many grams of trifle would have to be burned to raise the temperature of 1000 g of water by 2°C?

    A   1   B   2   C   3   D   4

5   Chocolate ice cream contains 9 kJ/g. Which of the activities in Table 7.2, when carried out for 30 minutes, uses the same amount of energy as is contained in 125 g of chocolate ice cream?

	activity	energy used (kJ/min)
A	playing football	37.5
B	walking up stairs	38.5
C	rowing	40.5
D	running	42.5

Table 7.2

6   Which of the following equations represents the regeneration of ATP from its components?

    A   ATP $\xrightarrow{\text{energy taken in}}$ $ADP + P_i$

            (high energy state)   (low energy state)

    B   ATP $\xrightarrow{\text{energy released}}$ $ADP + P_i$

            (low energy state)   (high energy state)

    C $ADP + P_i$ $\xrightarrow{\text{energy taken in}}$ ATP

            (low energy state)   (high energy state)

    D $ADP + P_i$ $\xrightarrow{\text{energy released}}$ ATP

            (high energy state)   (low energy state)

7   The following list gives examples of some cellular activities.

    1   synthesis of DNA

    2   transmission of nerve impulses

    3   division of a cell into two daughter cells

    4   contraction of skeletal muscle fibres

    Which of these require energy from the breakdown of ATP?

    A   1 and 3 only   B   2 and 4 only   C   1, 3 and 4 only   D   1, 2, 3 and 4

8   Which of the following would contain the LOWEST relative number of mitochondria?

    A   neuron   B   liver cell   C   cheek epithelial cell   D   skeletal muscle cell

9   Figure 7.2 shows the first stage in the biochemical pathway of respiration.

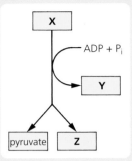

Figure 7.2

Which row in Table 7.3 correctly identifies the answers to boxes X, Y and Z?

	X	Y	Z
A	glucose	2 ATP	pyruvate
B	pyruvate	2 ATP	glucose
C	lactic acid	38 ATP	pyruvate
D	glucose	38 ATP	lactic acid

Table 7.3

Questions 10 and 11 refer to Figure 7.3 which shows the aerobic breakdown of pyruvate.

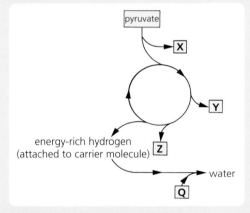

Figure 7.3

Questions 10 and 11 also refer to the following possible answers.

   A glucose   **B** oxygen   **C** lactic acid   **D** carbon dioxide

10 Which substance is released at positions X, Y and Z?

11 Which substance enters the system at point Q?

Questions 12, 13 and 14 refer to the data in Table 7.4, which were obtained from an athlete during training.

activity	mean volume of each breath (l)	rate of breathing (breaths per minute)	volume of air breathed per minute (l)
resting	0.5	12	6
jogging	1.5	24	36
running a race	box X	36	90

Table 7.4

12 The correct answer to box X is
  A 2.0   **B** 2.5   **C** 3.0   **D** 3.5
13 The percentage increase in rate of breathing from resting to running a race is
  A 33   **B** 50   **C** 67   **D** 200
14 The ratio of volume of air (in litres) breathed per minute by the athlete running a race to that breathed during jogging to that breathed at rest was
  A 1:6:15   **B** 3:2:1   **C** 15:6:1   **D** 90:54:30

Questions 15 and 16 refer to the experiment shown in Figure 7.4. It was set up to measure an earthworm's rate of respiration. After 30 minutes, the coloured liquid in the experiment was returned to its original level by depressing the syringe plunger from point P to point Q.

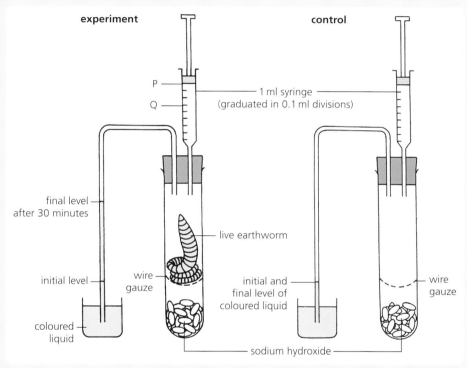

Figure 7.4

15 The rise in level of coloured liquid indicates that the
  A earthworm is taking in oxygen.
  B sodium hydroxide is absorbing oxygen.
  C earthworm is giving out carbon dioxide.
  D sodium hydroxide is releasing carbon dioxide.
16 From this experiment it can be concluded that the earthworm's rate of
  A oxygen consumption is 0.3 ml/hour.
  B oxygen consumption is 0.6 ml/hour.
  C carbon dioxide output is 0.3 ml/hour.
  D carbon dioxide output is 0.6 ml/hour.

17 As part of an investigation into aerobic respiration by germinating barley grains, the flasks shown in Figure 7.5 were set up and kept at 24°C. The hydrogen carbonate indicator changes colour from red to yellow in the presence of a relatively high concentration of carbon dioxide. In which flask did the indicator change colour first?

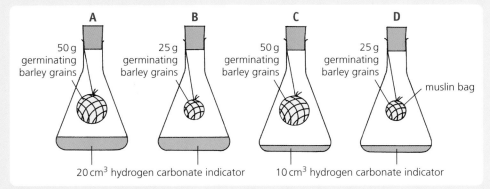

Figure 7.5

18 The apparatus shown in Figure 7.6 can be used to discover if soaked mung beans release carbon dioxide during respiration.

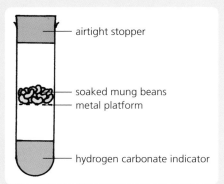

Figure 7.6

Which of the tubes shown in Figure 7.7 would be the most suitable control for this experiment?

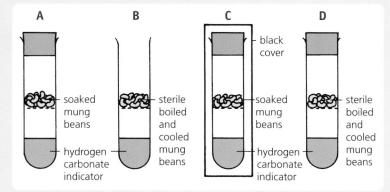

Figure 7.7

Questions 19, 20 and 21 refer to the graph in Figure 7.8. It shows the effect of a period of exercise, followed by a period of rest, on the lactic acid concentration of the blood of a healthy, fit teenager.

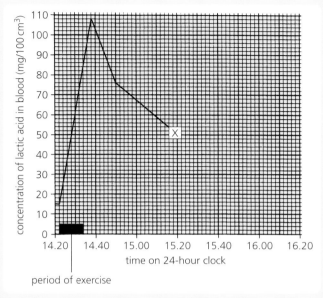

Figure 7.8

19 For how many minutes did the period of exercise last?
   A 6   **B** 10   **C** 12   **D** 14

20 How many minutes did it take for the concentration of lactic acid to drop from its highest level to 50% of its highest level?
   A 19   **B** 20   **C** 38   **D** 40

21 If the trend at X continues, at what time will the initial level of lactic acid in the blood be reached?
   A 15.56   **B** 16.02   **C** 16.08   **D** 16.20

22 Figure 7.9 represents the process of fermentation in plant cells.

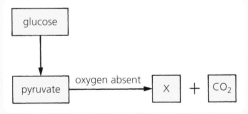

Figure 7.9

The substance released at position X is
   A ethanol   **B** oxygen   **C** hydrogen   **D** water

Questions 23 and 24 refer to Figure 7.10. It shows an experiment set up to investigate the effect of temperature on the rate of fermentation by yeast cells. Table 7.5 gives the results obtained.

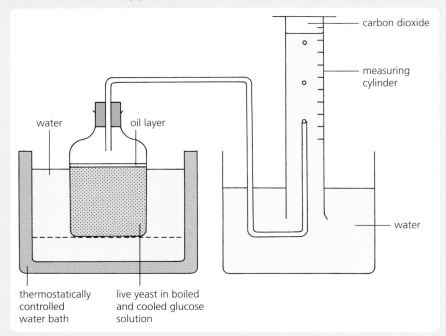

Figure 7.10

	temperature (°C)					
	10	**15**	**20**	**30**	**35**	**40**
mean volume (cm³) of CO_2 released per hour	4	11	16	34	43	45

Table 7.5

23 If the experiment were repeated at 25°C, the MOST likely mean volume (cm³) of CO_2 released per hour would be
   A 14   B 26   C 33   D 43
24 If the experiment were repeated at 70°C, the MOST likely mean volume (cm³) of CO_2 released per hour would be
   A 0   B 12   C 45   D 59
25 Which row in Table 7.6 is correct?

	respiration begins in the:		aerobic respiration is completed in the:		fermentation is completed in the:	
	cytoplasm	**mitochondria**	**cytoplasm**	**mitochondria**	**cytoplasm**	**mitochondria**
A	✔	✖	✔	✖	✖	✔
B	✖	✔	✖	✔	✔	✖
C	✖	✔	✔	✖	✖	✔
D	✔	✖	✖	✔	✔	✖

Table 7.6

(✔ = correct, ✖ = wrong)

8 Photosynthesis

Matching test
Match the terms in list X with their descriptions in list Y.

list X	list Y
1) ATP	a) by-product of photosynthesis that diffuses out of the cell
2) carbon dioxide	b) describing a factor whose restricted supply prevents an increase in the rate of a process
3) carbon fixation	c) soluble product of photosynthesis that contains chemical energy
4) cellulose	d) raw material that becomes split into oxygen and hydrogen during the first stage of photosynthesis
5) chemical	
6) chlorophyll	e) high energy compound that provides chemical energy needed to drive carbon fixation
7) chloroplast	f) a discus-shaped structure found in the cells of a green leaf
8) hydrogen	g) complex carbohydrate stored in plant cells
9) light	h) complex carbohydrate used to construct cell walls
10) light reactions	i) green pigment that traps light energy
11) limiting	j) form of energy trapped by chlorophyll for photosynthesis
12) oxygen	k) form of energy contained in sugar produced by photosynthesis
13) starch	l) raw material that supplies carbon atoms to be fixed into carbohydrate during photosynthesis
14) sugar	
15) water	m) processes that make up the first stage of photosynthesis
	n) series of enzyme-controlled reactions that make up the second stage of photosynthesis
	o) product of the splitting of water molecules during the light reactions that is needed for carbon fixation

Multiple choice test
Choose the ONE correct answer to each of the following multiple choice questions.

1 Which of the following word equations correctly represents the process of photosynthesis?
   A   water + carbon dioxide $\rightarrow$ sugar + oxygen + energy
   B   carbon dioxide + water + energy $\rightarrow$ sugar + oxygen
   C   sugar + carbon dioxide $\rightarrow$ water + oxygen + energy
   D   carbon dioxide + sugar + energy $\rightarrow$ water + oxygen

2 Which of the following terms refers to a green, discus-shaped structure found in a leaf cell?
   A starch   B cellulose   C chloroplast   D chlorophyll

3 During photosynthesis
   A   light energy is converted to chemical energy contained first in ATP and later in glucose.
   B   light energy is converted to chemical energy contained first in glucose and later in ATP.
   C   chemical energy is converted to light energy contained first in ATP and later in glucose.
   D   chemical energy is converted to light energy contained first in glucose and later in ATP.

$\rightarrow$

Questions 4 and 5 refer to Figure 8.1, which shows some of the steps carried out to test a leaf for the presence of starch.

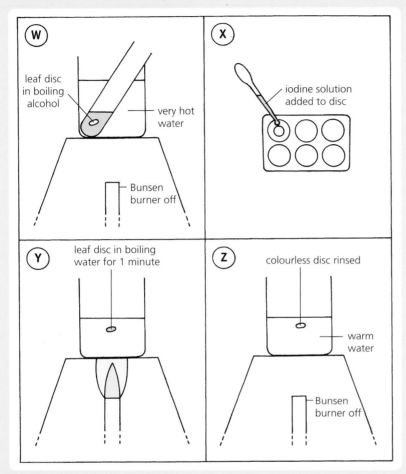

Figure 8.1

4 The correct sequence of steps is
   A Y, W, Z, X.   **B** Z, W, Y, X.   **C** Y, W, X, Z.   **D** Z, Y, W, X.

5 The reason for carrying out step W is to
   A kill the leaf cells.   **B** soften the leaf discs.
   C remove chlorophyll from the leaf cells.   **D** extract oxygen bubbles from the leaf discs.

6 The experiment shown in Figure 8.2 was set up to investigate if light is necessary for photosynthesis.

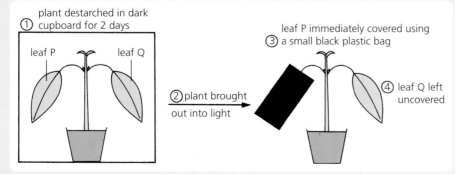

Figure 8.2

The validity of this experiment could have been increased by
A leaving leaf P uncovered.
B covering leaf Q with a black plastic bag.
C covering leaf Q with a transparent plastic bag.
D returning the whole plant to the dark cupboard.

7 The mean intensity of solar radiation falling on a crop of sugar cane plants was found to be 16 000 kJ/m²/day. If 4.5% of this energy was absorbed by the plants during photosynthesis, the number of kilojoules trapped per m² of plants per hour would be
A 30   B 720   C 3000   D 17 280

Questions 8 and 9 refer to the experiment shown in Figure 8.3. The plant was left in sunlight for 2 days and then leaf discs W, X, Y and Z were tested for the presence of starch.

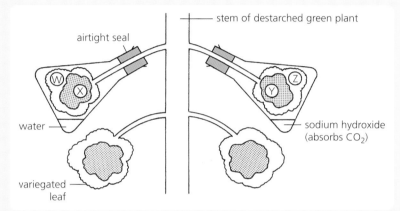

Figure 8.3

8 The leaf disc found to contain starch was
A W   B X   C Y   D Z

9 This experiment proves that in order to photosynthesise, a plant must have
A sunlight and carbon dioxide.   B carbon dioxide and water.
C chlorophyll and sunlight.   D carbon dioxide and chlorophyll.

10 The total volume of carbon dioxide daily entering the plant shown in Figure 8.4 is 24 000 mm³.

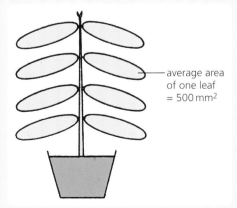

Figure 8.4

The daily rate of diffusion of carbon dioxide into the plant in mm³ CO_2 per mm² of leaf is
A 0.16   B 6   C 48   D 3000

Questions 11, 12 and 13 refer to Figure 8.5. It shows experiments set up to investigate which factors are necessary for photosynthesis.

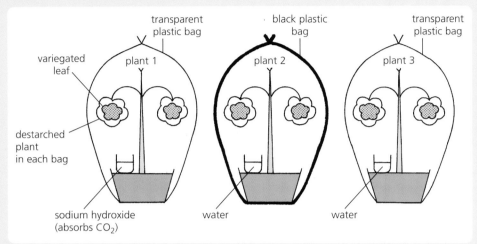

Figure 8.5

Questions 11, 12 and 13 also refer to the possible answers illustrated in Figure 8.6.

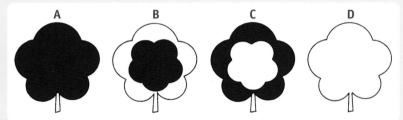

Figure 8.6

11 Which part of Figure 8.6 shows a leaf from plant 1 tested with iodine solution after 2 days?

12 Which part of Figure 8.6 shows a leaf from plant 2 tested with iodine solution after 2 days?

13 Which part of Figure 8.6 shows a leaf from plant 3 tested with iodine solution after 2 days?

14 The following three statements refer to possible uses to which carbohydrate, formed by photosynthesis, is put.

   1 Glucose is used as a source of energy.

   2 Cellulose is used to build cell walls.

   3 Excess sugar is stored as starch.

   Which of the statements are correct?

   A 1 and 2 only

   B 1 and 3 only

   C 2 and 3 only

   D 1, 2 and 3

15 Which of the following CANNOT be used to measure the rate of photosynthesis?

   A volume of oxygen released per unit time

   B volume of carbon dioxide taken up per unit time

   C mass of carbohydrate produced per unit time

   D volume of water vapour released per unit time

16 The graph in Figure 8.7 shows the results from a photosynthesis experiment.

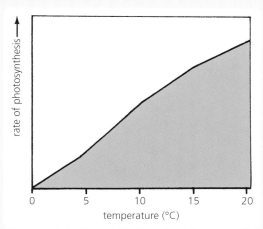

Figure 8.7

Which of the following pairs of environmental factors must be kept constant during this experiment to make it valid?
A light intensity and temperature
B temperature and carbon dioxide concentration
C water content and oxygen concentration
D light intensity and carbon dioxide concentration

Questions 17 and 18 refer to the graph in Figure 8.8. It shows the effect of increasing light intensity on the rate of photosynthesis by Canadian pondweed.

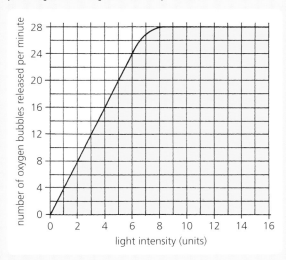

Figure 8.8

17 By how many times was the rate of photosynthesis at 8 units of light greater than that at 2 units of light?
A 3.5   B 4.0   C 20.0   D 224.0

18 What increase in the number of units of light intensity was required to double the rate of photosynthesis occurring at 3 units of light intensity?
A 3   B 6   C 12   D 24

19 Tables 8.1 and 8.2 refer to a survey done on the production of a certain crop plant in Scotland.

month seeds were sown	mean mass of crop produced (tonnes/hectare)
March	30
April	35
May	26

Table 8.1

number of plants grown per hectare	mean mass of crop produced (tonnes/hectare)
60 000	31
80 000	42
100 000	33

Table 8.2

Which combination of planting conditions shown in Table 8.3 would give the best crop yield?

	month seeds are sown	number of plants per hectare
A	April	60 000
B	March	80 000
C	April	80 000
D	May	100 000

Table 8.3

20 The graph in Figure 8.9 shows the effect of varying the CO_2 concentration at two different light intensities on the rate of photosynthesis by *Elodea*.

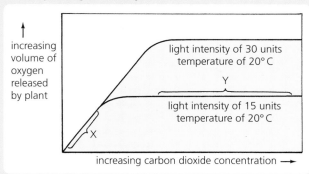

increasing volume of oxygen released by plant

light intensity of 30 units temperature of 20°C

Y

light intensity of 15 units temperature of 20°C

X

increasing carbon dioxide concentration →

Figure 8.9

Which row in Table 8.4 gives the factors that are limiting the rate of photosynthesis at regions X and Y on the graph?

	X	Y
A	light intensity	CO_2 concentration
B	light intensity	temperature
C	CO_2 concentration	light intensity
D	CO_2 concentration	temperature

Table 8.4

21 Early crops of tomatoes produced in greenhouses are often given extra carbon dioxide since the normal atmospheric concentration tends to act as a limiting factor. The additional carbon dioxide would be provided
  A during the night only since plants respire at night.
  B during the day only since photosynthesis occurs in light.
  C during the day and night since plants respire 24 hours a day.
  D on cloudy days only when light is a limiting factor.

22 Table 8.5 shows the results of a survey on the mass of food produced by a variety of plants as a result of photosynthesis.

	type of plant	mass of carbon fixed during season of most rapid growth (g/day)	mass of organic matter produced (tonnes/hectare/year)
	maize	8	25
A	spring wheat	10	22
B	swamp moss	7	23
C	seaweed	4	32
D	Scots pine	3	18

Table 8.5

Which type of plant in the table matches the following description? It is a form of natural vegetation and its daily rate of photosynthesis during its season of most rapid growth is less than that of maize yet its annual rate of food production exceeds that of maize.

23 Figure 8.10 shows four greenhouses set up to grow tomato plants. (The plants are not shown.)
In which greenhouse is the CO_2 concentration definitely the factor limiting photosynthesis?

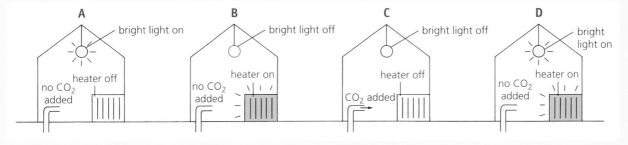

Figure 8.10

Questions 24 and 25 refer to the graph in Figure 8.11. It shows the effect of light intensity on the rate of photosynthesis at three different concentrations of carbon dioxide.

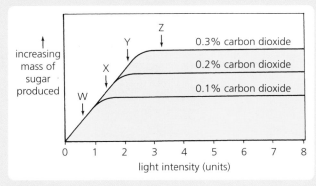

Figure 8.11

24 Which of the following light intensities was the limiting factor at all three concentrations of carbon dioxide?
   A 0–1 units   **B** 1–2 units   **C** 2–3 units   **D** 3–4 units

25 Carbon dioxide concentration was the limiting factor at
   A point W only.   **B** point Z only.   **C** points X and Y only.   **D** points W, X, Y and Z.

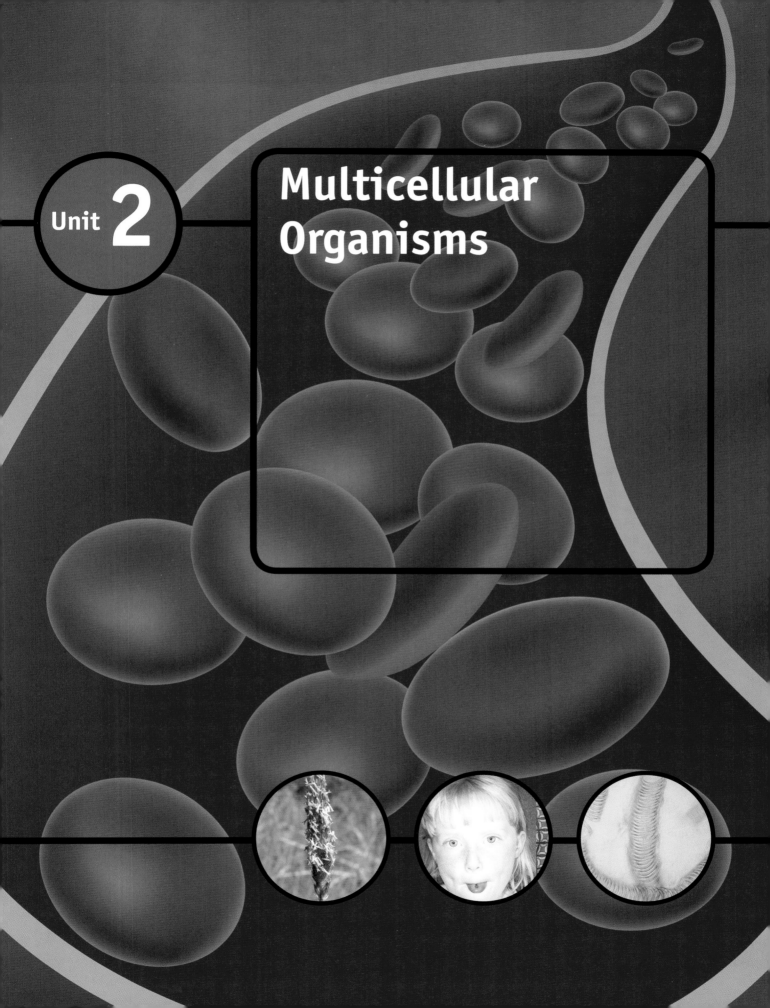

Unit 2

Multicellular Organisms

9 Cells, tissues and organs

Matching test
Match the terms in list X with their descriptions in list Y.

list X
1) blood
2) cell
3) ciliated epithelium
4) division of labour
5) multicellular
6) organ
7) root epidermis
8) specialised
9) system
10) tissue
11) unicellular
12) xylem

list Y
a) describing an organism whose body is composed of more than one cell
b) describing an organism whose entire body consists of one cell only
c) form of organisation where specific functions are carried out by groups of suitably specialised cells
d) animal tissue composed of cells specialised to transport oxygen and to defend the body
e) animal tissue composed of cells specialised to secrete mucus and to sweep dirty mucus up and away from the lungs
f) plant tissue composed of cells specialised to give protection and to absorb water
g) plant tissue composed of dead cells in the form of tubes specialised to give support and to transport water
h) basic unit of life
i) general name for a group of cells specialised to perform a particular function
j) structure composed of several different tissues that work together to perform one or more functions
k) group of related tissues and organs that work in close coordination to carry out one or more functions
l) state of cells that are structurally suited to perform a specific function

Multiple choice test
Choose the ONE correct answer to each of the following multiple choice questions.

1 Which of the following structures is the smallest unit that can lead an independent life?
  A atom   B cell   C nucleus   D organelle

Questions 2, 3 and 4 refer to Figure 9.1. It shows different types of cell from the human body.

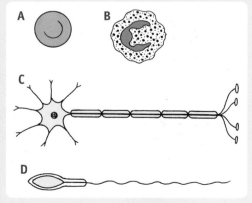

Figure 9.1

2 Which cell's structure is suited to the function of transmitting nerve impulses?
3 Which cell's structure is suited to the function of oxygen uptake?
4 Which cell's structure is suited to digesting and destroying bacteria that invade the body?
5 The function of goblet cells present in ciliated epithelium in the human trachea is to
  A release carbon dioxide.   B sweep microbes away.
  C secrete mucus.   D absorb oxygen.

6 Which of the following tubes present in the human body is lined with ciliated epithelium?

   A oviduct   **B** artery   **C** intestine   **D** vein

Questions 7, 8 and 9 refer to Figure 9.2. It shows different types of cells from a flowering plant.

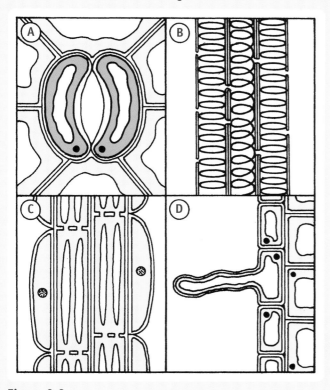

Figure 9.2

7 Which cell's structure is specialised to suit the function of water absorption from the external environment?

8 Which cell's structure is specialised to suit the function of support?

9 Which cell's structure is specialised to suit the function of controlling gaseous exchange between a leaf and the external environment?

10 Sieve tubes present in the phloem tissue of a plant possess sieve plates and a continuous stream of cytoplasmic strands. Therefore they are able to

   A carry water up the plant.

   B support the stem and leaves.

   C transport sugar down the plant.

   D exchange gases with surrounding tissues.

11 Figure 9.3 shows part of the human body.

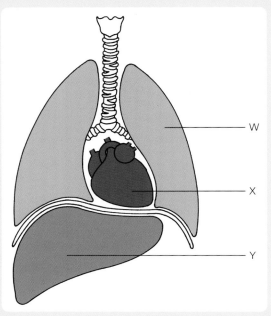

Figure 9.3

Which row in Table 9.1 matches organs W, X and Y with their functions?

	W	X	Y
A	pumping of blood	exchange of respiratory gases	breakdown of alcohol from bloodstream
B	exchange of respiratory gases	pumping of blood	maintenance of water balance
C	maintenance of water balance	breakdown of alcohol from bloodstream	pumping of blood
D	exchange of respiratory gases	pumping of blood	breakdown of alcohol from bloodstream

Table 9.1

12 Figure 9.4 shows a multicellular plant.

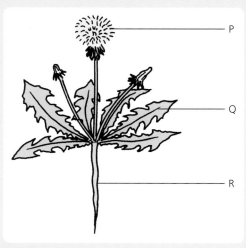

Figure 9.4

Which row in Table 9.2 matches organs P, Q and R with their functions?

	P	Q	R
A	gaseous exchange	photosynthesis	water absorption
B	reproduction	water absorption	gaseous exchange
C	reproduction	photosynthesis	water absorption
D	water absorption	support	reproduction

Table 9.2

13 Which type of organ in the human body is specialised to control water balance and remove soluble wastes?
   A skin   B kidney   C stomach   D large intestine
14 In a multicellular organism, an organ is composed of
   A a group of similar cells specialised to carry out a particular function.
   B several different types of cell that perform one function by a division of labour.
   C a group of related cells and systems that make up a complex tissue.
   D several different tissues that work together to carry out one or more functions.
15 Which of the following gives parts of the human body in the correct sequence of increasing complexity?
   A cell, tissue, organ, system, organism
   B organism, cell, tissue, system, organ
   C cell, tissue, system, organ, organism
   D organism, cell, system, tissue, organ

10 Stem cells and meristems

Matching test

Match the terms in list X with their descriptions in list Y.

list X	list Y
1) bone marrow	a) region of eye which, if damaged by chemical burning, can be treated using stem cells
2) cornea	b) technique used to replace the nucleus in an egg with a nucleus from a donor cell prior to stem cell production
3) embryonic	
4) ethics	c) moral values and rules that ought to govern human conduct
5) leukaemia	d) form of nuclear division which precedes cell division
6) meristem	e) state of a cell that has not become adapted to suit a specific function
7) mitosis	f) type of stem cell only able to replenish the supply of one or more specialised types of cell in the human body
8) non-specialised	
9) nuclear transfer	g) type of stem cell able to develop into all cell types found in the human body
10) stem	h) region of a plant containing non-specialised cells that have the potential to multiply and become different types of cell
11) tissue	
	i) general term referring to unspecialised cells that have the potential to multiply and become different types of cell
	j) type of cancer of the blood often treated using bone marrow transplantation
	k) tissue containing stem cells that can be transplanted from one person to another

Multiple choice test

Choose the ONE correct answer to each of the following multiple choice questions.

1 Which row in Table 10.1 correctly identifies the blanks in the following paragraph?

Stem cells are __1__ cells involved in the growth and repair of the body. They multiply by repeated __2__ and cell division, and develop into __3__ cells when required to replace lost or damaged cells.

	blank 1	blank 2	blank 3
A	unspecialised	mitosis	specialised
B	unspecialised	transplantation	specialised
C	specialised	mitosis	unspecialised
D	specialised	transplantation	unspecialised

Table 10.1

2 Table 10.2 refers to two types of stem cell.

	type of stem cell	types of cell that can be produced by stem cell
1	tissue	all types found in the human body
2	tissue	a few types closely related to the stem cell's source tissue
3	embryonic	all types found in the human body
4	embryonic	a few types closely related to the stem cell's source tissue

Table 10.2

Which rows in Table 10.2 are correct?

A 1 and 3   B 1 and 4   C 2 and 3   D 2 and 4

3 Figure 10.1 shows four stages involved in a type of nuclear transfer technique.

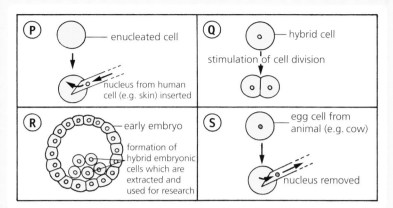

Figure 10.1

The correct order of these stages is

A   S, P, R, Q   B   P, S, Q, R   C   S, P, Q, R   D   P, S, R, Q

4   Table 10.3 shows the results of an investigation into the effect of a growth-stimulating chemical on a type of stem cell.

time (days)	number of viable stem cells x 10^5 per cm^3	
	flask X	flask Y
0	6.0	6.0
2	8.3	9.7
4	18.1	12.1
6	21.8	5.8
8	31.2	4.0
10	63.0	1.5

Table 10.3

Which row in Table 10.4 is correct?

	percentage increase in stem cell number after 10 days in flask X	percentage decrease in stem cell number after 10 days in flask Y
A	950	25
B	950	75
C	1050	25
D	1050	75

Table 10.4

5   The use of stem cells raises several ethical issues. 'Ethics' refers to the
   A   moral values that ought to govern human conduct.
   B   techniques followed when a procedure is closely regulated.
   C   safety standards that must be maintained during research work.
   D   qualifications of the experts employed to carry out stem cell investigations.

6 Meristematic cells
   A are only found at root tips.
   B give rise to various types of cell.
   C conduct water up to the leaves of a plant.
   D transport sugar down through the plant's stem.
7 The following steps are parts of the procedure employed to enable a root tip's meristem to be viewed under a microscope.
   1 root tip cells' chromosomes stained using purple acetic orcein.
   2 root tip cut off and fixed in warm hydrochloric acid
   3 root tip squashed to one cell thick under a coverslip
   4 root tip rinsed thoroughly in warm water
   The correct order in which these steps would be carried out is
   A 1, 2, 4, 3
   B 2, 4, 1, 3
   C 1, 3, 2, 4
   D 2, 1, 3, 4
8 Figure 10.2 shows the outcome of marking a bean seed's root with ink at regular intervals and allowing it to grow for a few days.

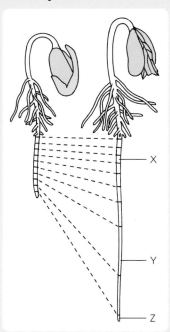

Figure 10.2

Which line in Table 10.5 correctly identifies regions X, Y and Z of the young root?

	region of elongation	region of mitosis	region of specialisation
A	X	Y	Z
B	Y	X	Z
C	Z	X	Y
D	Y	Z	X

Table 10.5

9 Figure 10.3 shows the shoot tip of a multicellular plant. Which site would contain specialised cells?

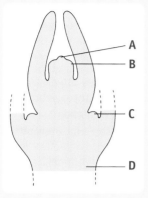

Figure 10.3

10 Under optimum growing conditions a bamboo shoot was found to increase in length by 22.68 inches in one day. What was the shoot's mean growth rate in mm/min?
(Note: 1 inch = 25.4 mm)

A 0.4   B 0.8   C 24.0   D 576.1

11 Control and communication

Matching test
Match the terms in list X with their descriptions in list Y.

list X
1) cerebellum
2) cerebrum
3) endocrine
4) glucagon
5) glycogen
6) hormone
7) insulin
8) medulla
9) motor neuron
10) receptor protein
11) reflex action
12) reflex arc
13) relay (inter) neuron
14) sensory neuron
15) synapse

list Y
a) type of nerve cell that carries nerve impulses from receptors in sensory organs to the CNS
b) type of nerve cell that carries impulses from a sensory neuron to a motor neuron
c) type of nerve cell that carries impulses from the CNS to muscles or glands
d) simple arrangement of three neurons that enables a nerve impulse to be transmitted from a receptor to an effector
e) tiny space between two neurons which briefly contains a chemical during the transmission of a nerve impulse
f) rapid, automatic, involuntary response to a stimulus
g) chemical messenger secreted into the blood by an endocrine gland
h) type of ductless gland that produces and secretes one or more hormones into the bloodstream
i) type of molecule present on a target tissue's cells specific to a particular hormone
j) hormone which activates the enzyme that promotes the conversion of glucose to glycogen
k) hormone which activates the enzyme that promotes the conversion of glycogen to glucose
l) storage carbohydrate composed of glucose
m) largest region of the brain responsible for mental processes
n) region of the brain responsible for balance and muscular coordination
o) region of the brain responsible for control of breathing and heart rate

Multiple choice test
Choose the ONE correct answer to each of the following multiple choice questions.

Questions 1, 2, 3, 4, 5, and 6 refer to Figure 11.1 of the human brain.

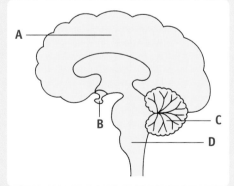

Figure 11.1

1 Which region is the cerebellum?
2 Which region is the medulla?
3 Which letter indicates the cerebrum?
4 Which region of the brain is responsible for higher mental faculties such as reasoning and imagination?
5 Which letter points to the region of the brain responsible for regulating heart beat?
6 When a certain region of the brain is affected by excessive consumption of alcohol, the person's movements become clumsy and uncoordinated. Identify this region of the brain.

7 Which part of Figure 11.2 correctly represents the flow of information through the nervous system?

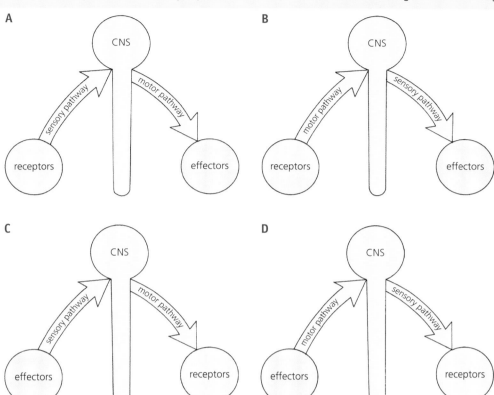

Figure 11.2

Questions 8 and 9 refer to Figure 11.3. It shows a simple reflex arc.

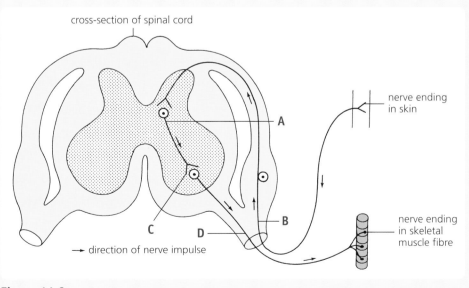

Figure 11.3

8 Which lettered structure indicates a sensory nerve fibre?

9 Which lettered structure represents a motor nerve fibre?

10 A reflex action is a rapid,
  A voluntary response to a stimulus.
  B involuntary response to a stimulus.
  C voluntary stimulus to a response.
  D involuntary stimulus to a response.
11 Which of the following statements refers correctly to a reflex action?
  A The stimulus is originally picked up by a relay neuron.
  B The effector responds on receiving nerve impulses from a motor neuron.
  C The nerve impulse always passes from receptor to effector via the brain.
  D The nerve impulse is passed from the motor to the sensory neuron.

Questions 12 and 13 refer to Tables 11.1 and 11.2.

reflex action	stimulus	response	protective function
dilation of eye pupil	P	contraction of certain iris muscles	Q
constriction of eye pupil	R	contraction of certain iris muscles	S

Table 11.1

	stimulus	protective function
A	dim light	prevents damage to the eye
B	dim light	improves vision in poor lighting
C	bright light	prevents damage to the eye
D	bright light	improves vision in poor lighting

Table 11.2

12 Which row in Table 11.2 provides the answers to blank boxes P and Q in Table 11.1?
13 Which row in Table 11.2 provides the answers to blank boxes R and S in Table 11.1?

Questions 14, 15 and 16 refer to Table 11.3.

reflex action	stimulus	response	protective function
A	harmful object approaching eye surface	contraction of eyelid muscle	prevents damage to eye
B	presence of food in gut	contraction of muscle in gut wall	ensures movement and efficient digestion of food
C	heat from naked flame	contraction of flexor muscle	moves limb to safety
D	foreign particles in nasal tract	sudden contraction of chest muscles	removes unwanted particles from inside of nose

Table 11.3

14 Which row in the table refers to sneezing?
15 Which row in the table refers to blinking?
16 Which row in the table refers to limb withdrawal?

17 Which row in Table 11.4 identifies the blanks in the following paragraph?

In addition to the part played by the nervous system, some control of the body is brought about by chemical messengers called __1__ released into the bloodstream by __2__ glands. This type of chemical messenger stimulates a target tissue which bears specific __3__ proteins on its cell surfaces.

	blank 1	blank 2	blank 3
A	neurons	digestive	effector
B	hormones	digestive	effector
C	neurons	endocrine	receptor
D	hormones	endocrine	receptor

Table 11.4

18 Which line in Table 11.5 correctly refers to the series of events that would occur in the body of a healthy non-diabetic person?

	concentration of glucose in blood	hormone made by pancreas	chemical reaction promoted
A	too low	insulin	glycogen → glucose
B	too low	glucagon	glucose → glycogen
C	too high	insulin	glucose → glycogen
D	too high	glucagon	glycogen → glucose

Table 11.5

19 Glucose tolerance is the capacity of the body to deal with ingested glucose. It is used as a test to diagnose diabetes. The graph in Figure 11.4 shows the responses of four people after ingesting a standard mass of glucose. Which person is most likely to be an untreated sufferer of type 1 diabetes?

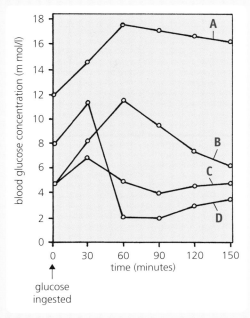

Figure 11.4

20 Anti-diuretic hormone (ADH) is secreted by the pituitary gland. This hormone regulates the water concentration of the blood by controlling the quantity of water reabsorbed into the blood from kidney tubules. These events are shown in Figure 11.5.

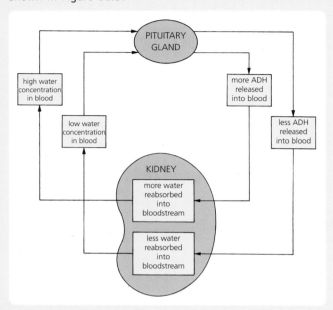

Figure 11.5

Which row in Table 11.6 gives the series of events that occurs if excess salt is consumed?

	water concentration of blood	quantity of ADH secreted by pituitary	quantity of water reabsorbed into bloodstream	volume of urine produced
A	↑	↑	↓	↓
B	↓	↑	↑	↓
C	↓	↓	↓	↑
D	↑	↓	↑	↑

Table 11.6

(↑ = increased, ↓ = decreased)

12 Reproduction

Matching test
Match the terms in list X with their descriptions in list Y.

list X	list Y
1) anther	a) term describing a body cell which contains two matching sets of chromosomes
2) diploid	b) term describing a sex cell which contains a single set of chromosomes
3) egg	c) general name for a haploid sex cell
4) fertilisation	d) tiny male gamete consisting of a head region (containing a nucleus) and a tail
5) gamete	e) process by which the nucleus of a male gamete fuses with that of a female gamete to form a zygote
6) gonad	
7) haploid	f) female gamete from an animal containing a nucleus and a store of food
8) ovary	g) general name for a reproductive organ in an animal that produces gametes
9) oviduct	h) site of production of sperm in animals
10) ovules	i) site of production of eggs in animals and flowering plants
11) pollen grains	j) normal site of fertilisation in a human female
12) pollination	k) site of production of pollen grains in flowering plants
13) sperm	l) product of fertilisation when the nuclei of two gametes fuse
14) testis	m) transfer of pollen from an anther to the stigma of a flower
15) zygote	n) microscopic structures containing a flowering plant's male sex cells
	o) tiny structures containing a flowering plant's female sex cells

Multiple choice test
Choose the ONE correct answer to each of the following multiple choice questions.

1 On average, the length of a human sperm is 0.06 mm. Expressed in micrometres, this would be

  A 6   B 60   C 600   D 6000

Questions 2 and 3 refer to Figure 12.1. It shows the human male reproductive system.

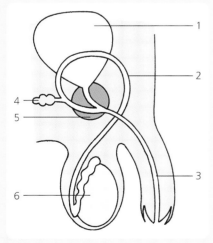

Figure 12.1

2 Sperm are produced in

  A 1   B 4   C 5   D 6

3 The routine male sterilisation operation known as vasectomy is carried out by

  A collapsing 1   B cutting 2   C blocking 3   D removing 6

4 On average, the diameter of a human egg is 120 μm. Expressed as a fraction of a millimetre, this would be

A 0.0012   **B** 0.012   **C** 0.12   **D** 1.2

5 Release of an egg from a gonad is called

A ovulation.   **B** ejaculation.   **C** gestation.   **D** menstruation.

Questions 6, 7 and 8 refer to Figure 12.2. It shows the human female reproductive system.

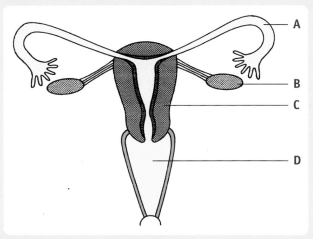

Figure 12.2

6 Which letter is pointing to the uterus?

7 Which part is the ovary?

8 In which region does fertilisation normally occur?

Questions 9, 10 and 11 refer to Figure 12.3. It shows part of a foxglove flower.

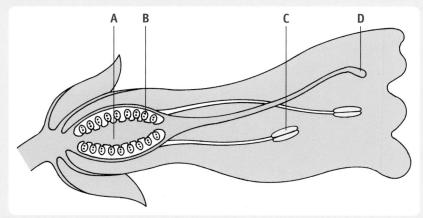

Figure 12.3

9 Which letter indicates the location of an egg cell?

10 Which letter shows the site of pollen grain production?

11 Which letter indicates the point where a zygote could be formed?

Questions 12 and 13 refer to Figure 12.4. It represents the human life cycle.

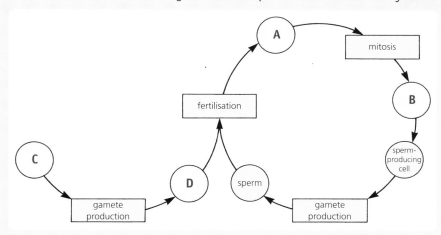

Figure 12.4

12 Which letter represents an egg?

13 Which letter represents a zygote?

Questions 14 and 15 refer to the bar graph in Figure 12.5. It shows the results of an extensive survey into the mean number of eggs laid in one year by various types of duck in Scotland.

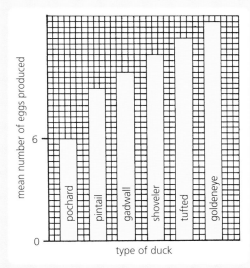

Figure 12.5

14 Which type of duck was found to lay a mean number of 12 eggs?

  A pintail   **B** gadwall   **C** tufted   **D** goldeneye

15 What was the mean number of eggs laid by the shoveler duck?

  A 13   **B** 12   **C** 11   **D** 10

13 Variation and inheritance

Matching test
Match the terms in list X with their descriptions in list Y.

list X
1) alleles
2) continuous
3) discrete
4) dominant
5) family tree
6) gene
7) genotype
8) heterozygous
9) homozygous
10) phenotype
11) polygenic
12) recessive

list Y
a) member of a pair of alleles that is always masked by the dominant allele
b) member of a pair of alleles that always shows its effect and masks the presence of the recessive allele
c) physical and biochemical characteristics of an organism resulting from the expression of its genes
d) the complete set of genes possessed by an organism
e) genotype that possesses two identical alleles of a particular gene
f) genotype that possesses two different alleles of a particular gene
g) a pedigree chart showing the occurrence of an inherited characteristic through several generations of related individuals
h) type of inheritance where a characteristic is controlled by several genes
i) form of variation shown by a characteristic which shows a smooth gradation of values from a minimum to a maximum
j) form of variation shown by a characteristic which can be used to divide members of a species into two or more distinct groups
k) basic unit of inheritance, many of which make up a chromosome
l) alternative forms of a gene that are responsible for different expressions of an inherited characteristic

Multiple choice test
Choose the ONE correct answer to each of the following multiple choice questions.

1 Which of the following is an example of continuous variation?
   A eye colour in fruit flies
   B diameter of shell in limpets
   C fingerprint type in humans
   D coat colour in guinea pigs

2 Which of the following is an example of discrete variation in humans?
   A length of foot   B ability to roll tongue   C rate of heartbeat   D circumference of head

Questions 3 and 4 refer to the following possible answers.
   A allele   B gamete   C genotype   D phenotype

3 Which term means the total set of genes possessed by an organism?
4 Which term means the physical appearance of an organism?

Questions 5 and 6 refer to Figure 13.1. It shows crosses involving tomato plants.

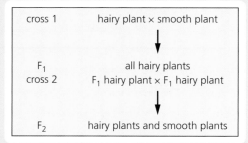

cross 1   hairy plant × smooth plant

F₁   all hairy plants
cross 2   F₁ hairy plant × F₁ hairy plant

F₂   hairy plants and smooth plants

Figure 13.1

5   The number of different genotypes present in the F_2 generation is
   A   1   B   2   C   3   D   4
6   If F_1 hairy plants are crossed with smooth plants, then a possible result for the offspring could be
   A   1000 hairy and 0 smooth.   B   756 hairy and 244 smooth.
   C   666 hairy and 334 smooth.   D   492 hairy and 508 smooth.
7   In pea plants, the allele for flower colour (H) is dominant to the allele for lack of flower colour (h). A plant homozygous for flower colour was crossed with a plant bearing colourless flowers. The F_1 plants were then self-pollinated.
   Which of the following correctly represents the ratio of genotypes expected in the F_2 generation?
   A   all Hh   B   1 HH:1 hh   C   3 HH:1 hh   D   1 HH:2 Hh:1 hh
8   In fruit flies, the allele for normal grey body colour (G) is dominant to the allele for ebony body colour (g). Table 13.1 summarises the results of several crosses.

cross	result
strain 1 × gg	all grey
strain 2 × gg	1 grey:1 ebony
strain 3 × gg	all ebony
strain 4 × Gg	3 grey:1 ebony

Table 13.1

Which strains BOTH have the genotype Gg?
   A   1 and 3   B   1 and 4   C   2 and 3   D   2 and 4

Questions 9 and 10 refer to Figure 13.2. It shows a series of crosses carried out using leopards.

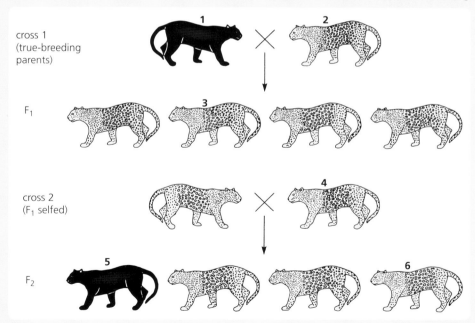

Figure 13.2

9   Which animal is definitely heterozygous with respect to the gene for coat type?
   A   1   B   2   C   3   D   5
10 Which animal is definitely homozygous with respect to the gene for coat type?
   A   3   B   4   C   5   D   6

11 In mice, black coat colour (allele B) is dominant to brown coat colour (allele b). The offspring of a cross between a black mouse (BB) and a brown mouse were allowed to interbreed. What percentage of the progeny would be expected to have black coats?

A   25   B   50   C   75   D   100

Questions 12 and 13 refer to the following information.

In pea plants, the gene for height has two alleles, tall (T) and dwarf (t). The cross shown in Figure 13.3 was carried out and then a further generation of pea plants was produced by allowing the first filial generation to self-pollinate.

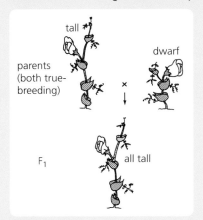

Figure 13.3

12 Which of Tables 13.2 shows a Punnett square that represents the second cross?

A

		genotypes of pollen	
		T	T
genotypes of eggs	t	tT	tT
	t	tT	tT

B

		genotypes of pollen	
		T	t
genotypes of eggs	T	TT	Tt
	t	tT	tt

C

		genotypes of pollen	
		T	t
genotypes of eggs	T	TT	TT
	t	tt	tt

D

		genotypes of pollen	
		t	t
genotypes of eggs	T	Tt	Tt
	T	Tt	Tt

Tables 13.2

13 The phenotypic ratio of tall to dwarf amongst the offspring of the second cross would be

A   1:1   B   2:1   C   3:1   D   4:1

14 Table 13.3, in the form of a Punnett square, shows the results of crossing organisms with genotype Rr where R is the dominant allele and r the recessive allele of a gene.

		male gametes	
		R	r
female gametes	R	1	2
	r	3	4

Table 13.3

Which TWO boxes represent organisms that would have the same phenotype but different genotypes?

A   1 and 2   B   2 and 3   C   1 and 4   D   3 and 4

15 In humans, an ability to roll the tongue (T) is dominant to an inability to roll the tongue (t). A woman who is a tongue-roller marries a man who is a non-roller. They have four children. One son and one daughter are tongue-rollers and one son and one daughter are non-rollers. Which of the family trees in Figure 13.4 correctly represents this information?

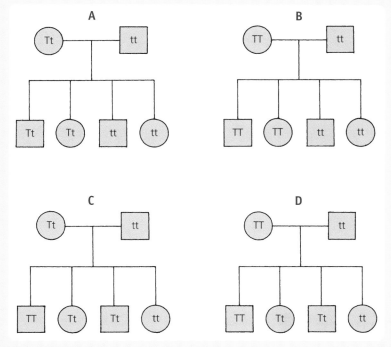

Figure 13.4

Questions 16 and 17 refer to the family tree shown in Figure 13.5 and to the following information.
In humans, the allele for red hair (h) is recessive to the allele for non-red hair (H).

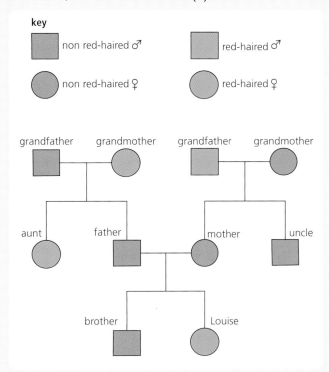

Figure 13.5

16 Which row in Table 13.4 is correct?

	genotype of Louise	genotype of Louise's parents
A	homozygous	heterozygous
B	homozygous	homozygous
C	heterozygous	homozygous
D	heterozygous	heterozygous

Table 13.4

17 Which row in Table 13.5 correctly identifies the genotypes of Louise's aunt and uncle?

	aunt	uncle
A	hh	HH
B	hh	Hh
C	Hh	hh
D	HH	Hh

Table 13.5

Questions 18 and 19 refer to Figure 13.6. It shows a family tree where the allele for wavy hair (W) is dominant to the allele for straight hair (w).

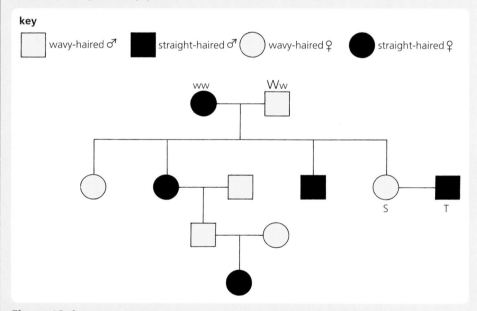

Figure 13.6

18 Which of the following statements is true about persons S and T?
   A They differ in both phenotype and genotype.   B They differ in phenotype but have the same genotype.
   C They have the same phenotype and the same genotype.   D They have the same phenotype but differ in genotype.
19 What is the chance of persons S and T producing a straight-haired child?
   A 1 in 1   B 1 in 2   C 1 in 3   D 1 in 4
20 A pattern of polygenic inheritance is based on a characteristic that shows
   A continuous variation and is affected by environmental factors.
   B continuous variation but is unaffected by environmental factors.
   C discrete variation and is affected by environmental factors.
   D discrete variation but is unaffected by environmental factors.

14 Transport systems in plants

Matching test
Match the terms in list X with their descriptions in list Y.

list X
1) companion cell
2) epidermis
3) guard cell
4) lignin
5) mesophyll
6) phloem
7) potometer
8) root hair
9) sieve plate
10) sieve tube
11) stoma
12) transpiration
13) vein
14) xylem

list Y
a) one of a pair of cells which change shape and control gaseous exchange by opening and closing stomata
b) one of many tiny pores found mainly on the lower leaf surfaces of non-grasslike plants
c) long extension of a root epidermal cell which presents a large surface area for water absorption
d) non-living tissue containing hollow, lignified vessels responsible for support and water transport in a plant
e) tough supporting material present as rings or spirals in xylem vessel walls
f) loss of water by evaporation from the aerial parts of a plant
g) live tissue responsible for sugar transport in a plant and composed of sieve tubes and companion cells
h) live component of phloem tissue which is controlled by a companion cell
i) live component of phloem tissue possessing a nucleus which controls the workings of a sieve tube
j) apparatus used to measure rate of water uptake by a plant and approximate rate of transpiration
k) branch of a leaf's transport system containing xylem and phloem tissues
l) layer of protective tissue on upper and lower surfaces of a leaf
m) end wall of a sieve tube perforated with holes that allow continuity of cytoplasm from tube to tube
n) tissues composed of green cells which comprise the plant's principal site of photosynthesis

Multiple choice test
Choose the ONE correct answer to each of the following multiple choice questions.

1 Figure 14.1 shows a close-up of part of a root. Which location contains cell sap of the highest water concentration?

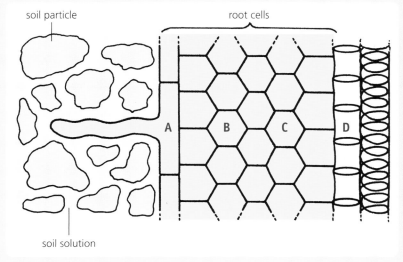

Figure 14.1

Questions 2 and 3 refer to the experiment shown in Figure 14.2. The cut end of a leafy shoot has been immersed for 1 hour in red dye and then a cross section cut at point X on the stem.

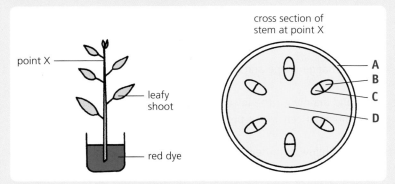

Figure 14.2

2   Which tissue would contain most red dye?

3   In which tissue would most dissolved sugar be found?

Questions 4, 5 and 6 refer to Figure 14.3. It shows a cross section through part of a green leaf.

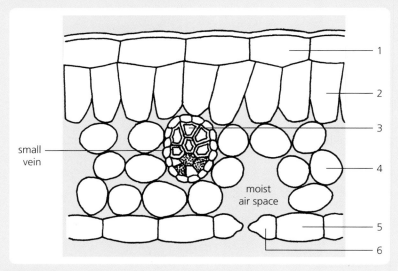

Figure 14.3

4   At which location is the water concentration highest?
   A 2   **B** 3   **C** 4   **D** 6

5   Chloroplasts would be present in ALL of cell types
   A 1, 2 and 4   **B** 2, 4 and 5   **C** 2, 4 and 6   **D** 4, 5 and 6

6   Which number indicates a palisade mesophyll cell?
   A 1   **B** 2   **C** 4   **D** 5

7   When a freshly picked leaf from a geranium plant is immersed in very hot water, many tiny bubbles appear on its lower surface and a few appear on its upper surface.
   Which of the following statements best explains this observation?
   A   There are more stomata in the leaf's upper epidermis than its lower epidermis.
   B   The pores in the leaf's upper surface respond to heat by closing.
   C   There are more stomata in the leaf's lower epidermis than its upper epidermis.
   D   The pores in the leaf's lower surface respond to heat by closing.

8 Which of the following is a possible route taken by water molecules as they pass through a leaf before being lost as water vapour to the external environment?

A xylem → spongy mesophyll → moist air space → stoma
B xylem → moist air space → spongy mesophyll → stoma
C spongy mesophyll → xylem → moist air space → stoma
D spongy mesophyll → xylem → stoma → moist air space

9 Figure 14.4 shows an experiment set up to investigate if water is lost from leaves of an Aspidistra plant.

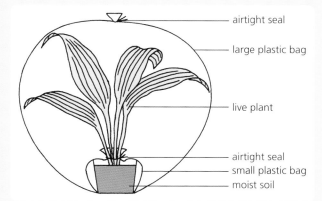

Figure 14.4

Which of the set-ups in Figure 14.5 would be the best control for the experiment?

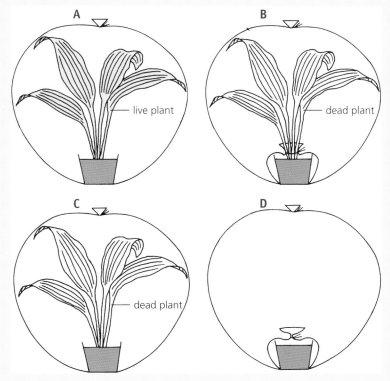

Figure 14.5

10 Each part of Figure 14.6 shows a pair of guard cells, either in light or dark. Which part is correct?

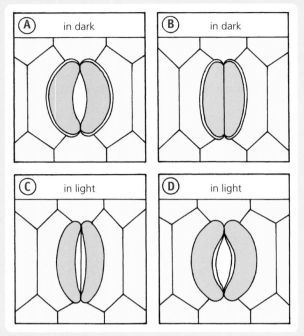

Figure 14.6

11 The graph in Figure 14.7 charts the rate of transpiration from a geranium plant's leaves. When did the plant's stomata begin to open?

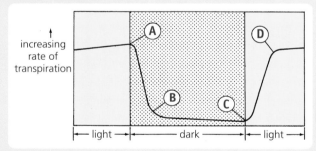

Figure 14.7

Questions 12 and 13 refer to Figure 14.8 which shows a bubble potometer.

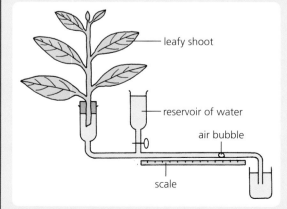

Figure 14.8

12 Which of the following is NOT an essential precaution taken when setting up and using this apparatus?

A   cutting the plant shoot under water

B   ensuring that the entire system is kept airtight

C   using a plant that bears both leaves and flowers

D   preventing the air bubble from reaching and entering the shoot

13 The bubble in a bubble potometer moves most rapidly when the leafy shoot is in conditions which are

A   light and windy.   B   dark and windy.   C   light and still.   D   dark and still.

Questions 14 and 15 refer to the experiment shown in Figure 14.9. It was set up to measure the rate of water loss from a leafy shoot at different light intensities. Table 14.1 shows the mean results from several repeats of the experiment.

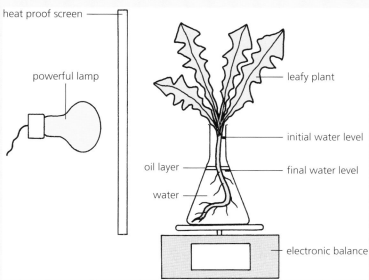

Figure 14.9

light intensity (units)	mean mass of water lost (g/h)
10	13
15	15
20	18
25	20
30	22
35	22
40	22

Table 14.1

14 From these results it can be concluded that the stomata were fully open at a light intensity of

A   15 units.   B   20 units.   C   25 units.   D   30 units.

15 The apparatus was left for 10 minutes at each new light intensity before taking measurements in order to

A   allow the plant to equilibrate to each new light intensity.

B   improve the reliability of the results for each new condition of light.

C   allow the plant to become acclimatised to changes in temperature.

D   ensure that only one variable factor was being altered at a time.

Questions 16 and 17 refer to the following information. In an investigation, a large leafy shoot was attached to a bubble potometer (see Figure 14.8 for diagram) and subjected in turn to each of eight treatments. These are summarised in Figure 14.10. In each case, the time taken by the bubble to travel a standard distance was recorded.

① 5°C		② 5°C	
light	RH 75%	dark	RH 95%
③ 25°C		④ 25°C	
light	RH 75%	dark	RH 95%
⑤ 5°C		⑥ 5°C	
dark	RH 75%	light	RH 95%
⑦ 25°C		⑧ 25°C	
dark	RH 75%	light	RH 95%

(Note: RH = relative humidity)

Figure 14.10

16 Which of the following pairs of treatments, on being compared, would allow a valid conclusion to be drawn about the effect of an environmental factor on the bubble's rate of movement?

    A 2 and 5   **B** 1 and 8   **C** 3 and 4   **D** 6 and 7

17 Which of the following pairs of treatments, on being compared, would NOT allow a valid conclusion to be drawn about the effect of an environmental factor on the bubble's rate of movement?

    A 1 and 5   **B** 2 and 4   **C** 3 and 8   **D** 4 and 6

18 Figure 14.11 shows an experiment involving four similar leaves that have been treated differently.

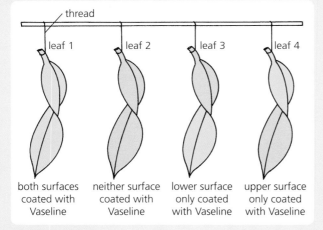

both surfaces coated with Vaseline   neither surface coated with Vaseline   lower surface only coated with Vaseline   upper surface only coated with Vaseline

Figure 14.11

After 3 days in light, the percentage loss in mass of each leaf was calculated. Which row in Table 14.2 gives the MOST likely set of results?

	percentage loss in mass			
	leaf 1	leaf 2	leaf 3	leaf 4
A	14	0	11	3
B	0	14	11	3
C	14	0	3	11
D	0	14	3	11

Table 14.2

19 Table 14.3 compares xylem with phloem. Which row is NOT correct?

	xylem	phloem
A	dead	alive
B	composed of sieve tubes and companion cells	composed of hollow vessels
C	supported by rings or spirals of lignin	not supported by rings or spirals of lignin
D	transports water up the plant	transports sugar up and down the plant

Table 14.3

20 'Ringing' is the name given to the process by which a band of outer tissues containing the phloem is peeled away from the stem of a plant while leaving the plant intact. Figure 14.12 shows a branch on an apple tree which is about to be ringed at points R and S.

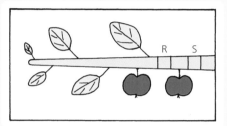

Figure 14.12

Which part of Figure 14.13 shows the correct appearance of this branch after several weeks of growth?

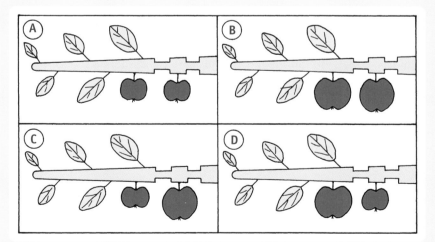

Figure 14.13

15 Animal transport and exchange systems

Matching test 1
Match the terms in list X with their descriptions in list Y.

list X	list Y
1) aorta	a) upper chamber of the heart that receives deoxygenated blood from the body
2) artery	b) upper chamber of the heart that receives oxygenated blood from the lungs
3) capillary	c) lower chamber of the heart that pumps oxygenated blood into the aorta
4) coronary artery	d) lower chamber of the heart that pumps deoxygenated blood to the lungs
5) deoxygenated	e) structure present in the heart and in veins that prevents backflow of blood
6) haemoglobin	f) main artery which carries oxygenated blood from the heart to the body
7) left atrium	g) main vein which carries deoxygenated blood to the heart from the body
8) left ventricle	h) blood vessel which transports oxygenated blood from the lungs to the heart
9) oxygenated	i) blood vessel which transports deoxygenated blood from the heart to the lungs
10) pulmonary artery	j) general term for a vessel that carries blood towards the heart
11) pulmonary vein	k) general term for a vessel that carries blood away from the heart
12) red blood cell	l) tiny thin-walled blood vessel in close contact with living cells
13) right atrium	m) biconcave disc that contains haemoglobin and transports oxygen
14) right ventricle	n) red pigment in red blood cells that combines with oxygen
15) valve	o) term used to describe blood that contains a high concentration of oxygen
16) vein	p) term used to describe blood that contains a low concentration of oxygen
17) vena cava	q) first branch of the aorta which supplies oxygenated blood to the muscular wall of the heart

Matching test 2
Match the terms in list X with their descriptions in list Y.

list X	list Y
1) alveolus	a) wavelike motion of gut wall caused by alternate contraction and relaxation of muscular wall
2) amino acids	b) one of many finger-like projections that increase the absorbing surface of the small intestine
3) bronchus	c) end product of digestion of complex carbohydrates such as starch
4) cartilage	d) building blocks of protein and end products of protein digestion
5) cilia	e) building blocks of fat molecules and end products of fat digestion
6) digestion	f) tiny lymph vessel inside a villus that absorbs fatty acids and glycerol
7) fat	g) region of gut from which end products of digestion are absorbed into the bloodstream
8) fatty acids and glycerol	h) breakdown of large insoluble particles of food into small soluble particles
9) glucose	i) energy-rich food composed of fatty acids and glycerol
10) lacteal	j) tough material laid down in incomplete rings that support the trachea
11) mucus	k) tube connecting the larynx with the bronchi and allowing entry and exit of air to and from the lungs
12) peristalsis	l) sticky substance secreted by cells lining the trachea that traps dirt and microorganisms
13) small intestine	m) hair-like projections on inner surface of the trachea that sweep dirty mucus upwards
14) trachea	n) tiny air sac with a thin lining that allows efficient gas exchange with the bloodstream
15) villus	o) branch of trachea that allows air to enter and leave a lung

Multiple choice test

Choose the ONE correct answer to each of the following multiple choice questions.

Questions 1, 2, 3 and 4 refer to Figure 15.1 which shows a mammalian heart.

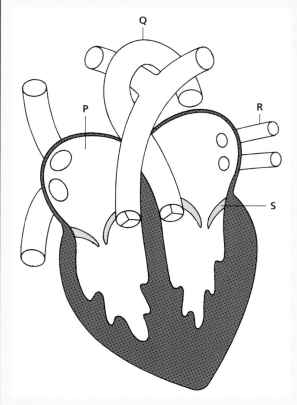

Figure 15.1

1 Chamber P is called the
  A left atrium and it receives blood from all parts of the body.
  B right atrium and it receives blood from the lungs.
  C left atrium and it receives blood from the lungs.
  D right atrium and it receives blood from all parts of the body.
2 Vessel Q carries
  A oxygenated blood away from the heart.
  B deoxygenated blood towards the lungs.
  C oxygenated blood away from the lungs.
  D deoxygenated blood towards the heart.
3 Vessel R is the
  A aorta.
  B vena cava.
  C pulmonary artery.
  D pulmonary vein.
4 The function of structure S is to
  A prevent oxygenated blood mixing with deoxygenated blood.
  B prevent oxygenated blood passing from a ventricle to an atrium.
  C direct the flow of deoxygenated blood returning from the lungs.
  D direct the flow of deoxygenated blood from the heart to the lungs.

5　The coronary arteries supply

A oxygenated blood to the heart wall muscle.	B deoxygenated blood to the heart wall muscle.
C oxygenated blood to the ventricle chambers.	D deoxygenated blood to the ventricle chambers.

6　Which row in Table 15.1 is correct?

	relative thickness of heart wall		reason for difference
	right ventricle (RV)	**left ventricle (LV)**	
A	thicker	thinner	RV pumps blood all round the body
B	thinner	thicker	LV pumps blood all round the body
C	thicker	thinner	LV pumps blood all round the body
D	thinner	thicker	RV pumps blood all round the body

Table 15.1

7　Figure 15.2 shows four diagrams of a mammalian heart. In which heart is the blood flowing in the correct direction?

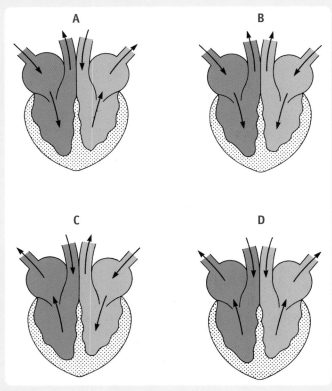

Figure 15.2

8　Which of the following differences between an artery and a vein is correct?

	feature	artery	vein
A	diameter of central cavity	narrow	wide
B	state of muscular wall	thin	thick
C	valves	present	absent
D	pressure of blood in vessel	low	high

Table 15.2

9 Which part of Figure 15.3 shows the correct sequence of the vessels in which blood is transported round the body?

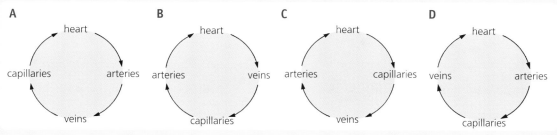

Figure 15.3

10 Which of the following is NOT true of the body's capillary network?
   A   It forms a dense network that serves all living cells.
   B   It consists of many arteries and veins in all body parts.
   C   The walls of its vessels are only one cell thick.
   D   The combined surface area of its vessels is enormous.

11 The graph in Figure 15.4 charts percentage saturation of haemoglobin with oxygen as the concentration of oxygen in its surroundings increases.

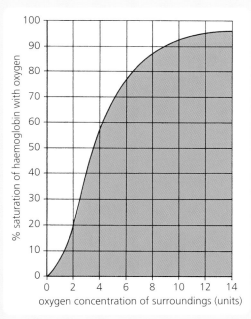

Figure 15.4

If haemoglobin, already acclimatised to surroundings of oxygen concentration 12 units, was transported to body tissues of oxygen concentration 3 units, it would off-load oxygen. The resulting decrease in its percentage saturation with oxygen would be

A 9   B 40   C 55   D 95

Questions 12, 13, 14 and 15 refer to the following information.

At high altitudes, the air is thinner and less oxygen is gained by the body per breath. Graphs 1 and 2 in Figure 15.5 refer to the altitudes reached by, and the red blood cell counts of, a group of climbers on a mountaineering expedition.

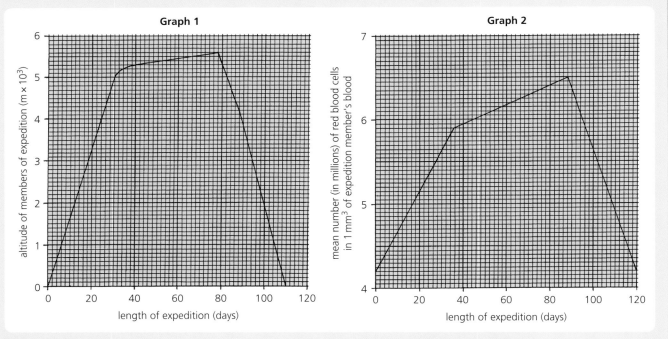

Figure 15.5

12 Which row in Table 15.3 gives the correct values for day 24?

	altitude reached (m x 10³)	number of red blood cells (millions per mm³)
A	4.0	5.35
B	4.7	5.55
C	4.0	5.55
D	4.7	5.35

Table 15.3

13 On which day did the climbers reach the highest altitude?
   A 78   B 79   C 84   D 88

14 How many days did the members of the expedition spend at an altitude of 5 x 10³ m or above?
   A 46   B 51   C 52   D 56

15 What was the mean number of red blood cells, in millions per mm³, present in a climber's blood on day 84?
   A 4.20   B 4.70   C 6.45   D 6.50

16 Which of the following gives the correct order of the structures through which air passes on being inhaled?
   A trachea, bronchus, bronchiole, alveolus   B bronchus, trachea, alveolus, bronchiole
   C trachea, bronchus, alveolus, bronchiole   D bronchus, trachea, bronchiole, alveolus

17 Which part of Figure 15.6 correctly represents gas exchange in a pair of air sacs in a human lung?

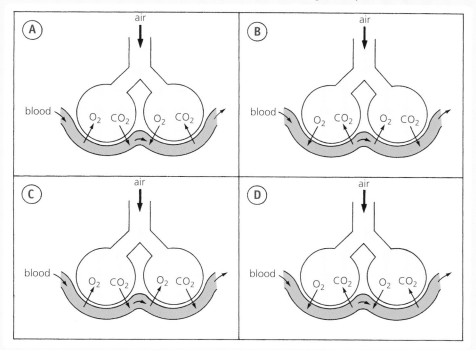

Figure 15.6

18 The following list gives four equations relating to haemoglobin. Which TWO are correct?

1   haemoglobin + oxygen $\xrightarrow{\text{in lungs}}$ oxyhaemoglobin

2   haemoglobin + oxygen $\xrightarrow{\text{in tissues}}$ oxyhaemoglobin

3   oxyhaemoglobin $\xrightarrow{\text{in lungs}}$ haemoglobin + oxygen

4   oxyhaemoglobin $\xrightarrow{\text{in tissues}}$ haemoglobin + oxygen

A   1 and 3   B   1 and 4   C   2 and 3   D   2 and 4

19 Various aspects of a woman's breathing were investigated. The results are shown in Table 15.4.

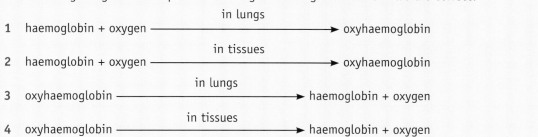

concentration of oxygen in inhaled air (%)	20
concentration of oxygen in exhaled air (%)	16
number of breaths per minute	15
average volume of each breath (cm^3)	500

Table 15.4

The volume of oxygen (in cm^3) absorbed by her lungs each minute was

A   20   B   300   C   1500   D   3000

20 Which part of Figure 15.7 correctly represents the process of peristalsis?

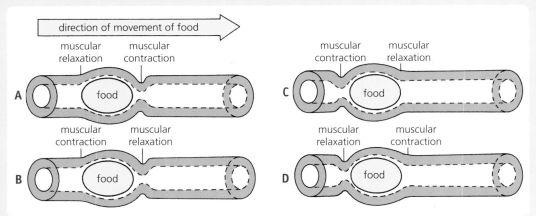

Figure 15.7

Questions 21, 22 and 23 refer to Figure 15.8. It shows a graph of data obtained during an experiment where a person's stomach contents were sampled before, during, and at regular intervals after a meal was eaten.

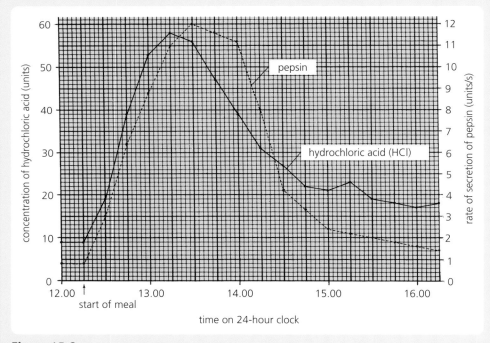

Figure 15.8

21 Which row in Table 15.5 correctly records the concentrations of the two substances at 14.15?

	HCl (units)	pepsin (units/s)
A	6.2	40.0
B	16.5	4.4
C	22.0	3.3
D	31.0	8.0

Table 15.5

22 The number of minutes taken by pepsin to drop from its maximum rate of secretion to 5 units per second was
   A 19   B 55   C 57   D 59
23 The time at which 44 units of hydrochloric acid and 11.4 units per second of pepsin were recorded was
   A 12.51   B 13.21   C 13.51   D 13.57

Questions 24 and 25 refer to Figure 15.9. It shows a close-up of the surface of a small intestine.

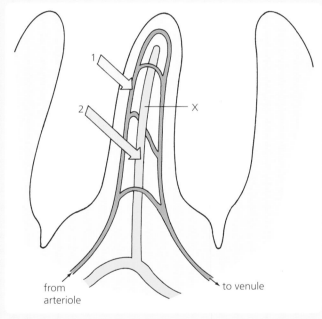

Figure 15.9

24 Structure X is called
   A a lacteal.
   B a goblet cell.
   C an epithelium.
   D a blood capillary.
25 The products of protein digestion enter by route
   A 1 and are transported in the lymphatic system.
   B 2 and are transported in the blood circulatory system.
   C 2 and are transported in the lymphatic system.
   D 1 and are transported in the blood circulatory system.

16 Effects of lifestyle choices

Matching test
Match the terms in list X with their descriptions in list Y.

list X
1) alcohol
2) cancer
3) carbon monoxide
4) diabetes
5) exercise
6) heart attack
7) mental
8) obese
9) physical
10) reaction time
11) stroke

list Y
a) term used to describe a person who is excessively overweight
b) physical exertion especially for the purpose of keeping fit
c) interval of time between detecting a stimulus and responding to it
d) intoxicating liquid which is harmful to the liver and brain when consumed to excess
e) term used to describe the aspect of health that refers to parts of the body such as heart, lungs and liver
f) term used to describe the aspect of health that refers to the person's state of mind and emotional wellbeing
g) blockage or bursting of a blood vessel in the brain that may cause permanent damage to brain tissue
h) disorder characterised by a blood glucose level that is much higher than the normal level
i) abnormal growth (tumour) caused by uncontrolled division of cells
j) damage to heart muscle resulting from blockage of a blood vessel and lack of oxygen
k) poisonous gas present in cigarette smoke that combines with haemoglobin reducing its capacity to transport oxygen

Multiple choice test
Choose the ONE correct answer to each of the following multiple choice questions.

Questions 1, 2 and 3 refer to the Table 16.1, which shows how a healthy lifestyle can help people to avoid certain serious illnesses. Each tick counts as a score of one positive point towards avoiding the illness.

serious illness	beneficial aspect of lifestyle					
	diet rich in fruit and vegetables	diet low in salt	diet low in fat	regular exercise daily	no smoking	little or no alcohol
heart attack	✔✔	✔	✔✔✔	✔✔✔	✔✔✔	
liver cancer	✔✔					✔✔✔
lung cancer	✔		✔		✔✔✔	
stroke	✔✔	✔✔✔		✔✔	✔	

Table 16.1

(no tick = zero reduction of risk of suffering illness

✔ = minor reduction of risk of suffering illness

✔✔ = medium reduction of risk of suffering illness

✔✔✔ = major reduction of risk of suffering illness)

1 The risk of one of the serious illnesses is reduced to a major extent by eating a diet low in salt. Which illness?

  A heart attack   **B** liver cancer   **C** lung cancer   **D** stroke

2 The risk of two of the illnesses is reduced to a major extent by not smoking. Which two?

  A heart attack and lung cancer

  B lung cancer and liver cancer

  C liver cancer and stroke

  D stroke and heart attack

3 Which aspect of a healthy lifestyle makes a minor contribution to reducing the risk of a heart attack?
   A a diet low in salt
   B a diet rich in vegetables
   C a diet rich in fruit
   D a diet low in fat
4 Which person in Table 16.2 is most likely to suffer high blood pressure?

person	overweight?	junk food eaten regularly?	regular exercise taken?	stress-free lifestyle?
A	✔	✔	✘	✔
B	✔	✔	✘	✘
C	✘	✘	✔	✔
D	✘	✔	✘	✘

Table 16.2

(✔ = yes, ✘ = no)

Questions 5 and 6 refer to the graph in Figure 16.1. It records the pulse rate of a woman taken at 1-minute intervals before, during and after a period of vigorous exercise.

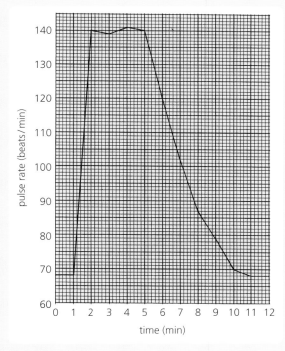

Figure 16.1

5 For how many minutes did the period of vigorous exercise last?
   A 1   B 2   C 3   D 4
6 During which time interval in minutes did pulse rate decrease at the fastest rate?
   A 5–6   B 6–7   C 7–8   D 8–9

Questions 7, 8 and 9 refer to the chart shown in Figure 16.2. It shows four levels of fitness targets and the rate at which the heart should be beating during exercise to reach these targets.

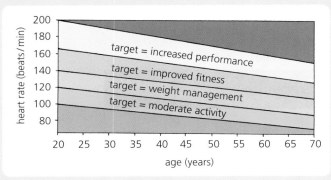

Figure 16.2

7 A 20-year-old woman wishes to increase her performance. Which range should her heart rate (in beats/min) be in while she is exercising?

   A 100–119   **B** 120–139   **C** 140–165   **D** 166–200

8 A 35-year-old woman exercised until her heart rate reached and stayed at around 120 beats/min. This was correct for the target she had set for herself. Identify the target.

   A increased performance   **B** weight management   **C** improved fitness   **D** moderate activity

9 A man aged 50 wishes to improve his fitness. While he is exercising, his heart rate (in beats/min) should be approximately

   A 100   **B** 120   **C** 140   **D** 160

10 The graph in Figure 16.3 charts a boy's pulse rate. Calculate his fitness index using the formula

$$\text{fitness index} = \frac{\text{length of exercise time (s)}}{\text{increase in pulse} \times \text{recovery time (min)}}$$

and then use Table 16.3 to find out his level of fitness.

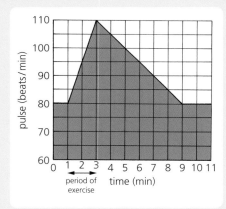

Figure 16.3

fitness index	level of fitness
3 or more	excellent
2–2.9	very good
1–1.9	good
0.5–0.9	fair
0.4 or less	unfit

Table 16.3

His level of fitness was

   A fair.   **B** good.   **C** very good.   **D** excellent.

11 Figure 16.4 shows a small portion of the coronary artery of a sufferer of angina. Which letter indicates a deposit of fatty material?

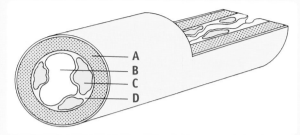

Figure 16.4

12 Table 16.4 shows some of the findings from a survey on the death rate from heart disease of people aged between 45 and 69 years.

country	deaths per 100 000 population	
	women	men
Japan	10	51
France	35	115
Germany	64	246
Australia	68	340
Scotland	140	510

Table 16.4

Which of the following statements is correct?

A Compared with Australian men, the death rate amongst Scottish men is 1.5 times lower.

B Compared with German women, the death rate amongst Scottish women is 3 times higher.

C Compared with Scottish women, the death rate amongst French women is 4 times lower.

D Compared with Scottish men, the death rate amongst Japanese men is 10 times higher.

Questions 13, 14 and 15 refer to the graph in Figure 16.5. It shows the effect of alcohol on a man's reaction time.

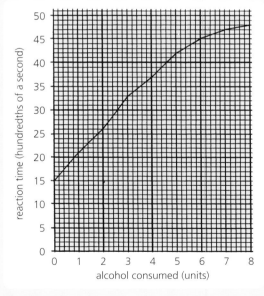

Figure 16.5

13 What was the man's reaction time (in hundredths of a second) after he had drunk two pints of beer each containing two units of alcohol?

    A 25.1   **B** 26.0   **C** 35.2   **D** 37.0

14 What was the increase in length of his reaction time (in hundredths of a second) when the alcohol that he consumed rose from 1 unit to 8 units?

    A 22   **B** 27   **C** 33   **D** 48

15 What was the percentage increase in the length of his reaction time when the alcohol that he consumed rose from 1 unit to 6 units?

    A 24.0   **B** 87.5   **C** 100.0   **D** 114.3

Questions 16, 17 and 18 refer to the bar chart in Figure 16.6. It is based on a survey of the number of cigarettes smoked daily and the death rates from coronary heart disease in British men.

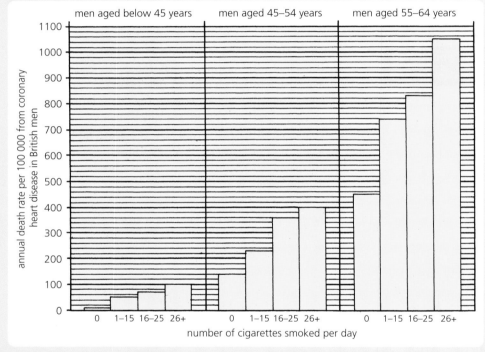

Figure 16.6

16 The annual death rate per 100 000 from coronary heart disease for 40-year-old men who smoke 20 cigarettes daily is

    A 70   **B** 85   **C** 100   **D** 360

17 An annual death rate of 400 per 100 000 from coronary heart disease is found for men aged

    A 45–54 who smoke 1–5 cigarettes daily.

    B 45–54 who smoke 16–25 cigarettes daily.

    C 45–54 who smoke 26+ cigarettes daily.

    D 55–64 who smoke 0 cigarettes daily.

18 Which of the following conclusions can be correctly drawn from the information in the bar chart?

    A Among men under the age of 45, only smokers die of coronary heart disease.

    B Men who smoke 30 cigarettes daily are four times more likely to suffer coronary heart disease when they are 50 than when they are 25.

    C The chance of dying of coronary heart disease decreases for men who survive beyond the age of 55 and still continue to smoke 10 cigarettes daily.

    D 60-year-old men who smoke 10 cigarettes daily are less likely to die of coronary heart disease than 50-year-old men who smoke 20 cigarettes daily.

Questions 19 and 20 refer to the graphs in Figure 16.7. They show the percentage of babies of different birth weights born in a hospital over a period of 1 year.

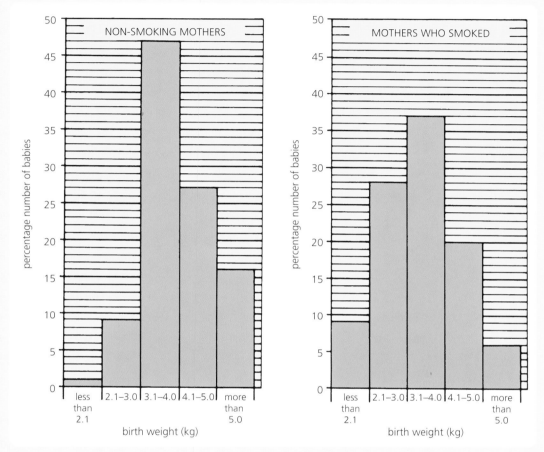

Figure 16.7

19 What percentage of babies born to mothers who smoked had birth weights in the range of 3.1–5.0 kg?

  A 37   **B** 47   **C** 57   **D** 74

20 Which row in Table 16.5 is correct?

	non-smoking mothers		mothers who smoked	
	percentage of babies that weighed:		**percentage of babies that weighed:**	
	3.0 kg or less	**3.1 kg or more**	**3.0 kg or less**	**3.1 kg or more**
A	9	47	28	37
B	10	90	37	63
C	37	63	10	90
D	28	37	9	47

Table 16.5

Unit 3

Life on Earth

17 Biodiversity and the distribution of life

Matching test
Match the terms in list X with their descriptions in list Y.

list X	list Y
1) abiotic	a) natural biological unit made up of living and non-living parts
2) biodiversity	b) struggle for existence between members of a community caused by the limited supply of an essential resource
3) biome	
4) biotic	c) loss of land to desert as a result of human activities
5) community	d) large region of the Earth distinguished from others by its climate, flora and fauna
6) competition	e) animal that is hunted by other animals
7) deforestation	f) all of the populations of plants, animals and microorganisms that live together in an ecosystem
8) desertification	
9) ecosystem	g) place in an ecosystem where an organism lives
10) habitat	h) role played by an organism within a community in an ecosystem
11) niche	i) ecological relationship where one organism, the parasite, benefits at the expense of another organism, the host
12) parasitism	
13) pollution	j) animal that hunts other animals for its food supply
14) population	k) general term for contamination of the environment
15) predator	l) complete clearing away of vast tracts of natural forest and the failure to renew them
16) prey	m) group of organisms of one species in an ecosystem
	n) term used to refer to a factor that relates directly to some aspect of living organisms in an ecosystem such as competition for food
	o) term used to refer to a factor that relates directly to a non-living feature of an ecosystem such as light intensity
	p) the total variation that exists among all the living things on Earth

Multiple choice test
Choose the ONE correct answer to each of the following multiple choice questions.

1 Biodiversity is best defined as the variation
   A that exists amongst the members of both sexes within a single species.
   B produced amongst the offspring of a cross between two members of a species.
   C that occurs amongst members of the same species adapted to different ecosystems.
   D found within and between all species present in the world's many different ecosystems.

Questions 2, 3 and 4 refer to the following possible answers.
   A niche   B habitat   C ecosystem   D community
2 Which term means the place where an organism lives?
3 Which term means a natural biological unit made up of living and non-living parts?
4 Which term refers to an organism's whole way of life and the use to which it puts the available environmental resources?
5 Which of the following is an example of an abiotic factor that affects the biodiversity in an ecosystem?
   A light intensity
   B competition for resources
   C disease among the community
   D grazing pressure on green plants
6 Which of the following is an example of a biotic factor that affects the biodiversity in an ecosystem?
   A pH   B moisture   C predation   D temperature

7 Table 17.1 shows the effect of pollution on the biodiversity of a river ecosystem.

	direction of flow of river water ⟶			
	state of water			
	clean	very badly polluted	partly polluted	clean
biodiversity present in ecosystem	large number of different species	very small number of different species	X	large number of different species

untreated sewage added

Table 17.1

Which of the following should have been inserted in box X in the table?

A small number of different species
B very small number of different species
C large number of different species
D very large number of different species

8 Figure 17.1 shows a type of ecosystem.

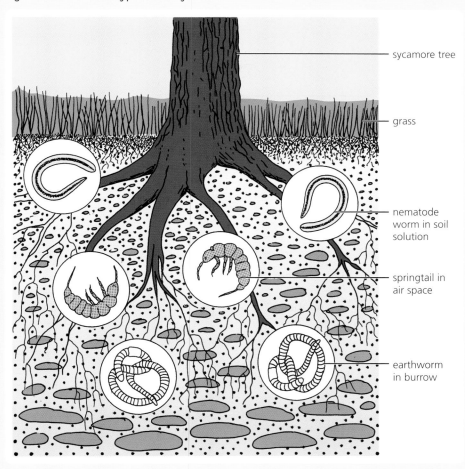

sycamore tree

grass

nematode worm in soil solution

springtail in air space

earthworm in burrow

Figure 17.1

Which of the following are BOTH examples of habitats?

A air space and soil solution

B burrow and earthworm

C springtail and earthworm

D soil solution and nematode worm

9 Which of the graphs shown in Figure 17.2 BEST represents a typical predator–prey relationship?

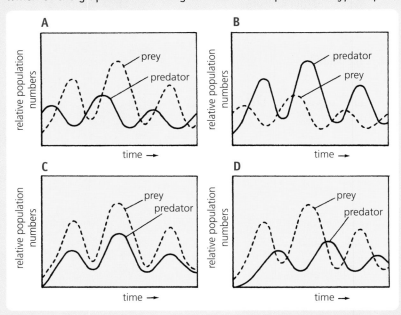

Figure 17.2

10 Some of the events that lead to desertification are listed below.

1 Forests are cleared and pastures are overgrazed.

2 Agricultural land is lost to advancing sand dunes.

3 The human population increases rapidly.

4 Topsoil dries out and is blown away.

The sequence in which these events occur is

A 1, 3, 2, 4   **B** 1, 3, 4, 2   **C** 3, 2, 1, 4   **D** 3, 1, 4, 2

11 Which of the following procedures would be LEAST likely to slow down the process of desertification?

A planting trees to act as a windbreak

B pursuing traditional farming practices such as crop rotation

C conserving resilient grasses that prevent soil erosion

D cultivating marginal land for crop-growing

Questions 12 and 13 refer to the chart in Figure 17.3. It shows the results of a survey into the effect of pH on the biodiversity of fish species in a freshwater loch.

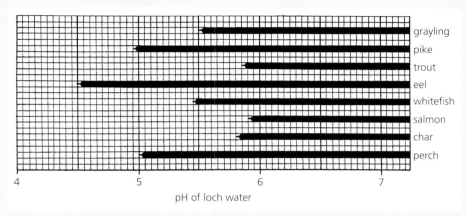

Figure 17.3

12 The number of species of fish that were found in loch water of pH 5.25 was

A 1   B 3   C 4   D 5

13 No salmon were found at pH

A 5.75   B 5.95   C 6.05   D 6.25

14 The graph in Figure 17.4 shows the results of a competition experiment between two species of animal (X and Y) that consume the same type of food.

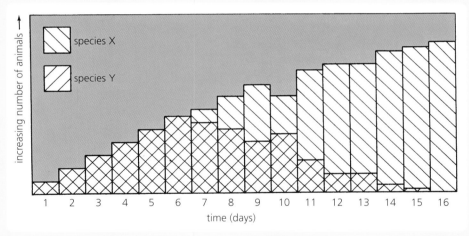

Figure 17.4

Species X was first found to be winning the competition at day

A 6   B 7   C 12   D 16

Questions 15 and 16 refer to the graph in Figure 17.5. It charts the results from a study of a predator and its well-fed prey.

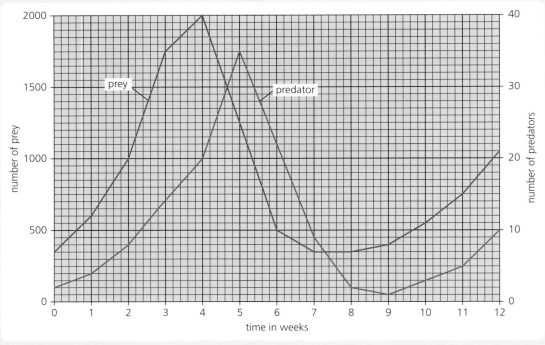

Figure 17.5

15 By how many individuals did the predator population increase in number from week 1 to week 5?
   A 31   B 33   C 1550   D 1650

16 By how many times did the prey outnumber the predators at week 4?
   A 2   B 25   C 100   D 1000

17 A large region of planet Earth which is distinguished from others by its climate, flora and fauna is called a
   A niche.   B continent.   C land mass.   D biome.

Questions 18 and 19 refer to the bar graphs in Figure 17.6. They show the number of species of vertebrate animals and vascular plants recorded in the years 1900 and 2000 for a large region of mainland Scotland.

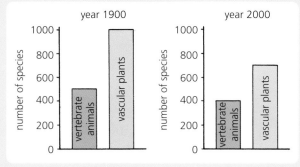

Figure 17.6

18 The percentage decrease in species number of each group is

	vertebrate animals	vascular plants
A	10	30
B	20	30
C	10	70
D	20	70

Table 17.2

19 The factor most likely to have been responsible for these changes in biodiversity is
   A global warming.   B gale-force winds.
   C agricultural intensification.   D glaciations during an ice age.

20 Grey seals were hunted so intensively before the *Grey Seal Protection Act* of 1914 that only about 1800 individuals remained in Scotland at that time. By 1999, Scotland possessed about 45% of the world's total grey seal population of 200 000. During the twentieth century the Scottish population of grey seals had increased by a factor of
   A 45   B 50   C 90   D 111

21 Which of the following is an economic reason for conserving biodiversity?
   A It is morally wrong to allow thousands of species to become extinct.
   B The successful functioning of natural balanced ecosystems requires stability.
   C It may be possible to develop new foods from wild varieties of plants.
   D The variety of wild life species helps to enrich the nation's landscape.

Questions 22 and 23 refer to Figure 17.7. It combines a line graph of temperature with a bar graph of rainfall for a biome of deciduous forest.

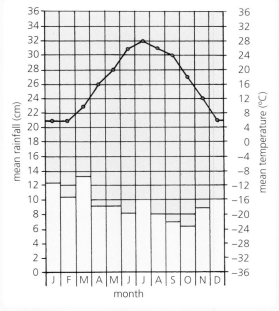

Figure 17.7

22 The two driest months of the year were
   A January and February.   B January and December.
   C February and December.   D September and October.

23 A biome of tropical forest was found to have a mean temperature of 27°C in March. By how many times was this value greater than the one for deciduous forest in March?
   A 1.2   B 2.7   C 3.0   D 17.0

24 Figure 17.8 shows a climograph for six different biomes.

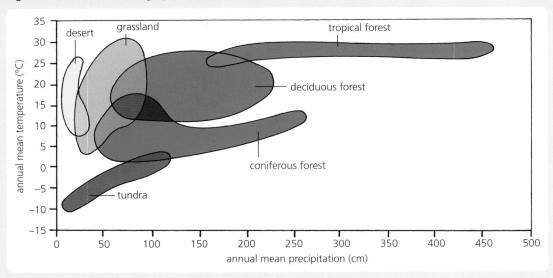

Figure 17.8

Which pair of values in Table 17.3 are both shared by three different biomes?

	mean annual precipitation (cm)	mean annual temperature (°C)
A	75	10
B	100	10
C	75	15
D	100	15

Table 17.3

25 Table 17.4 gives the mean net primary production of six biomes.

biome	mean net primary production (g/m²/y)
tropical rainforest	2100
evergreen forest	1400
deciduous forest	1200
savannah	910
grassland	630
tundra	140

Table 17.4

What is the whole number ratio of the mean net primary production of tropical rainforest to savannah to tundra?

A 15:10:1   B 30:13:2   C 15:9:2   D 30:20:1

18 Energy in ecosystems

Matching test
Match the terms in list X with their descriptions in list Y.

list X
1) carnivore
2) consumer
3) decomposers
4) decomposition
5) denitrification
6) food chain
7) herbivore
8) interspecific
9) intraspecific
10) nitrate
11) nitrification
12) nitrogen fixation
13) omnivore
14) primary consumer
15) producer
16) pyramid
17) root nodule
18) secondary consumer

list Y
a) general name for an organism unable to photosynthesise and dependent upon a ready-made food supply
b) herbivorous animal that eats the producer in a food chain
c) animal that eats the primary consumer in a food chain
d) diagram that indicates relative number, biomass or energy content of the organisms in a food chain
e) breakdown of dead organisms or waste material by microorganisms, releasing chemical nutrients back into the ecosystem
f) process by which certain bacteria in soil convert ammonium compounds to nitrite and nitrite to nitrate
g) process by which certain bacteria break down nitrate in the soil solution releasing nitrogen gas
h) process by which certain bacteria absorb nitrogen gas and convert it to ammonium compounds
i) swelling containing nitrogen-fixing bacteria found on roots of leguminous plants
j) microorganisms such as some types of fungi and bacteria that obtain their energy by breaking down dead organisms or waste material
k) compound containing nitrogen that is absorbed from the soil solution by plant roots and used to make protein
l) green plant which makes food by photosynthesis
m) energy-flow relationship starting with a green plant followed by a series of animals each of which feeds on the previous one
n) animal that feeds on plant material only
o) animal that eats both plant and animal material
p) animal that feeds on flesh and other animal material only
q) type of competition between members of the same species for the same resources in an ecosystem
r) type of competition between members of different species for the same resource(s) in an ecosystem

➡

Multiple choice test
Choose the ONE correct answer to each of the following multiple choice questions.

1   Figure 18.1 shows part of a seashore food web.

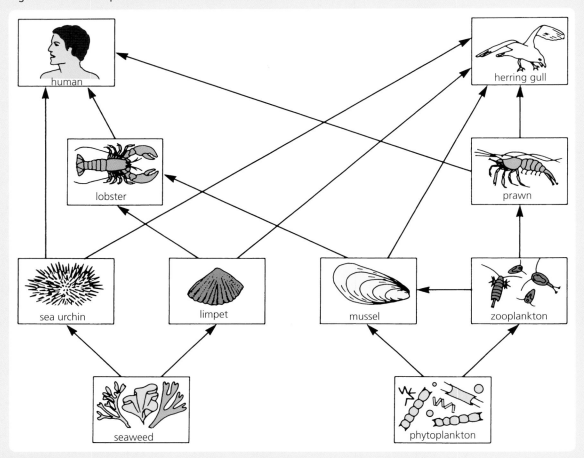

Figure 18.1

Which of the following food chains extracted from the seashore food web is NOT correct?

A   seaweed → limpet → lobster → human
B   phytoplankton → mussel → lobster → human
C   seaweed → sea urchin → lobster → herring gull
D   phytoplankton → zooplankton → prawn → herring gull

Questions 2, 3, 4 and 5 refer to Figure 18.2. It shows part of a food web in a freshwater pond.

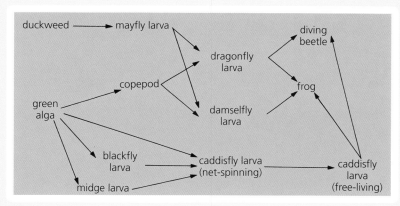

Figure 18.2

2 The number of different food chains that include dragonfly larva is

   A 1   **B** 2   **C** 3   **D** 4

3 An animal in this food web that is NOT eaten by other animals is

   A mayfly larva.   **B** copepod.   **C** midge larva.   **D** diving beetle.

4 An omnivore in this food web is

   A green alga.

   B blackfly larva.

   C caddisfly larva (free-living).

   D caddisfly larva (net-spinning).

5 If all the mayfly larvae were removed, it is very likely that the

   A duckweed population would decrease.

   B number of copepods would decrease.

   C number of damselfly larvae would increase.

   D number of dragonfly larvae would increase.

Questions 6 and 7 refer to the following information.

During a soil ecosystem investigation, certain members of the soil community were placed in containers like the one shown in Figure 18.3. The results are given in Table 18.1.

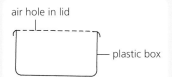

Figure 18.3

	box 1	box 2	box 3	box 4	box 5	box 6
organisms present at start	two lettuce roots and two centipedes	two lettuce roots and two leather-jackets	two lettuce roots and two millipedes	two ground beetles and two leather-jackets	two millipedes and two centipedes	two lettuce roots and two ground beetles
organisms present after 3 days	two lettuce roots and two centipedes	two leather-jackets	two millipedes	two ground beetles	two centipedes	two lettuce roots and two ground beetles

Table 18.1

6 Which of the following conclusions is NOT justified from these results?
   A Lettuce plants are producers and centipedes are secondary consumers.
   B Leather-jackets and millipedes are both primary consumers.
   C Millipedes and ground beetles are both preyed upon by centipedes.
   D Ground beetles are predators and leather-jackets are their prey.

7 The reliability of the results could be increased by
   A increasing the number of air holes in the lids of the boxes.
   B having only one primary consumer included in the experiment.
   C omitting the ground beetles from the investigation.
   D using a larger number of each type of soil organism.

Questions 8, 9 and 10 refer to Figure 18.4. It shows a loch food web.

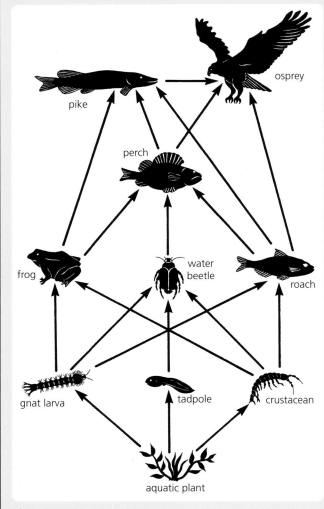

Figure 18.4

8 Which of the following are BOTH secondary consumers?
   A perch and frog
   B roach and perch
   C frog and water beetle
   D water beetle and tadpole

9 The number of different primary consumers in this food web is

  A 1   **B** 3   **C** 6   **D** 9

10 The population of organisms with the largest relative biomass would be

  A pike.   **B** perch.   **C** osprey.   **D** aquatic plants.

Questions 11 and 12 refer to Figure 18.5. It shows the number of units of energy in kJ/m^2 that were transferred from organism to organism in a grassland food chain.

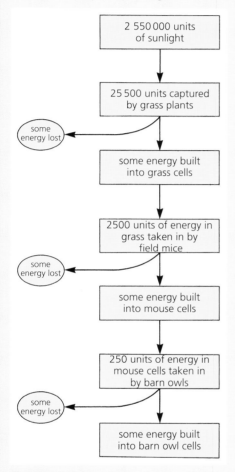

Figure 18.5

11 What percentage of sunlight energy was successfully captured by the grass?

  A 1   **B** 10   **C** 90   **D** 99

12 What percentage of energy was lost between 'intake of energy in grass by field mice' and 'intake of energy in mouse cells by barn owls'?

  A 1   **B** 10   **C** 90   **D** 99

13 The following list gives five food chains. If the biomass of the producer is equal in each, which TWO could support the largest number of human beings?

  1 wheat → human

  2 corn → cow → human

  3 rice → human

  4 corn → hen → human

  5 wheat → pig → human

  A 1 and 3   **B** 1 and 5   **C** 2 and 3   **D** 4 and 5

Questions 14 and 15 refer to the pie chart in Figure 18.6. It shows the daily energy balance of a laying hen.

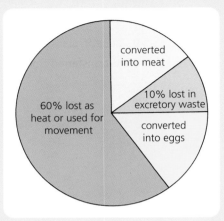

Figure 18.6

14 The percentage of the hen's energy intake that is converted into eggs is

   A 15   **B** 20   **C** 25   **D** 30

15 If the hen's daily total energy intake was 1220 kJ how many kilojoules were converted to meat?

   A 122   **B** 183   **C** 305   **D** 366

Questions 16 and 17 refer to the following food chain and to the four parts of Figure 18.7 which comprise a set of possible answers.

grass → gazelle → lion → flea

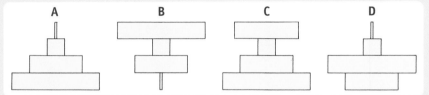

Figure 18.7

16 Which diagram best represents the food chain as a pyramid of numbers?

17 Which diagram best represents the food chain as a pyramid of energy?

18 A loch was stocked with 200 1-year-old trout each weighing, on average, 30 g. During the following year the trout increased in mass by 50% and then 40% of the trout were caught by fishermen. The total biomass in grams of trout remaining in the loch was

   A 1200   **B** 1800   **C** 3600   **D** 5400

19 Figure 18.8 shows a pyramid of biomass for an area of grassland.

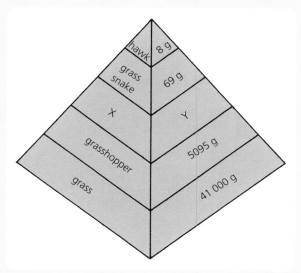

Figure 18.8

Which row in Table 18.2 gives the information missing from parts X and Y?

	X	Y
A	frog	570 g
B	magpie	570 g
C	frog	5705 g
D	magpie	5705 g

Table 18.2

Questions 20, 21 and 22 refer to Figure 18.9. It shows the circulation of nitrogen within an ecosystem.

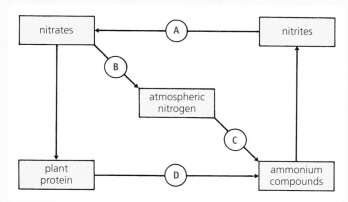

Figure 18.9

20 Which process represents the action of nitrifying bacteria?

21 Which process represents the action of free-living nitrogen-fixing soil bacteria?

22 Which process represents the action of denitrifying bacteria?

Questions 23 and 24 refer to the following information.

Galium saxatile grows best in acidic soil but will grow on alkaline soil in the absence of competition. *Galium pumilum*, on the other hand, grows best on alkaline soil but can survive on acidic soil.

In a competition experiment, equal numbers of seeds of both species of *Galium* were planted together in two pots. Pot 1 contained alkaline soil and pot 2 contained acidic soil.

23 Which of the sets of results shown in Table 18.3 is the most likely outcome of this experiment?

	pot 1 (alkaline soil)		pot 2 (acidic soil)	
	G. saxatile	*G. pumilum*	*G. saxatile*	*G. pumilum*
A	+	–	–	+
B	–	+	+	–
C	+	–	+	–
D	–	+	–	+

Table 18.3

(+ = growth, – = no growth)

24 This experiment involves
   A interspecific competition and one variable factor.
   B intraspecific competition and one variable factor.
   C interspecific competition and two variable factors.
   D intraspecific competition and two variable factors.

25 Table 18.4 gives the results from a plant competition experiment where five groups of pea plants were grown in areas of fertile soil measuring 0.25 m^2.

plant group	number of plants per 0.25 m^2	mean length of pod (mm)	mean number of pods per plant	mean number of seeds per pod	average mass of seed (g)
1	20	100	8.3	6.0	0.66
2	40	98	6.8	5.9	0.54
3	60	102	3.9	6.2	0.69
4	80	95	2.7	5.9	0.75
5	100	97	2.1	6.0	0.63

Table 18.4

From the data, which feature appears to be affected by competition between neighbouring pea plants?
A mean length of the pod
B mean number of pods per plant
C mean number of seeds per pod
D mean mass of seed

19 Sampling techniques and measurements

Matching test
Match the terms in list X with their descriptions in list Y.

list X
1) abiotic
2) abundance
3) beating
4) biotic
5) distribution
6) key
7) line transect
8) netting
9) pitfall trap
10) quadrat
11) randomisation
12) replication
13) sampling technique
14) source of error
15) Tullgren funnel

list Y
a) square-shaped sampling unit of known area
b) open container buried to its rim in soil and used to catch animals active on the soil surface
c) method used to sample an ecosystem at intervals along a straight line
d) means of identifying organisms based on their characteristics using a series of paired statements
e) term used to refer to a factor that relates directly to some aspect of living organisms in an ecosystem such as competition for food
f) term used to refer to a factor that relates directly to a non-living feature of an ecosystem such as light intensity
g) trap designed to catch tiny soil organisms by making them move away from hot, dry, bright conditions
h) method of obtaining data based on samples that are sufficient in number to be representative of the population or ecosystem as a whole
i) procedure by which several samples are taken at each sampling site to increase the reliability of the results
j) measure of the extent to which an organism occurs in an ecosystem (such as rare, common etc.)
k) sampling technique used to collect small animals from the branch of a tree
l) location or spread of a type of living organism in an ecosystem
m) sampling technique used to catch aquatic organisms
n) arrangement of samples that lacks a prearranged pattern in order to eliminate bias
o) limitation of a sampling technique that produces unreliable results

Multiple choice test
Choose the ONE correct answer to each of the following multiple choice questions.

Questions 1 and 2 refer to Figure 19.1. It gives a key to the percentage of different types of invertebrate animal that were caught in a collection of pitfall traps.

invertebrate animal	percentage	colour code
springtails	55	
beetles	25	
woodlice	12	
millipedes	6	
earthworms	2	

Figure 19.1

1   Which of the pie charts in Figure 19.2 correctly represents these data?

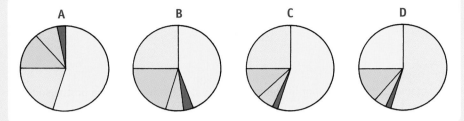

A   B   C   D

Figure 19.2

2   If the total number of animals collected was 300, how many of them were neither springtails nor woodlice?
    A 33   **B** 67   **C** 99   **D** 233

3   Figure 19.3 shows four Tullgren funnels set up to extract tiny animals from samples of the same freshly dug soil. Which trap is most likely to give the earliest results?

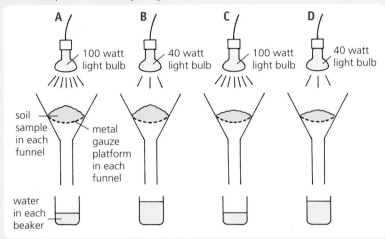

A   100 watt light bulb   B   40 watt light bulb   C   100 watt light bulb   D   40 watt light bulb

soil sample in each funnel   metal gauze platform in each funnel

water in each beaker

Figure 19.3

4   Figure 19.4 shows a 'safe' pooter used to capture small, slow-moving invertebrates.

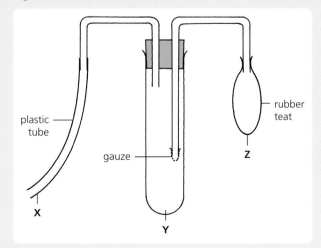

plastic tube

gauze

rubber teat

X

Y

Z

The following list gives the steps followed when using this pooter.
1   Insert X into area to be investigated.
2   Release pressure on Z.
3   Examine specimens trapped in Y.
4   Squeeze Z to expel air.
The correct order of the steps is
A   1, 4, 2, 3
B   4, 1, 2, 3
C   1, 4, 3, 2
D   4, 1, 3, 2

Figure 19.4

5 Which row in Figure 19.5 is NOT correct?

	ecosystem	sampling technique	equipment	possible source of error	way in which error may be minimised
A	soil	trapping	soil level / beaker	birds may eat the trapped animals	disguise the trap's opening with a lid supported on stones
B	pond	netting	water net	small animals may escape through holes in the net's mesh	rotate the handle of the net to close the opening after taking the sample
C	meadow	netting	sweep net	the number and types of animals caught may not be representative of the ecosystem as a whole	increase the number of sweep samples
D	tree	beating	stick / tray	some organisms may escape from the tray	quickly insert the tray into a large plastic bag and capture the specimens

Figure 19.5

6 Figure 19.6 represents a rocky shore. An abundance survey of the periwinkle population was carried out at sites W, X, Y and Z. The results are summarised in Table 19.1 where 0 = absent, 1 = rare, 2 = occasional, 3 = frequent and 4 = abundant.

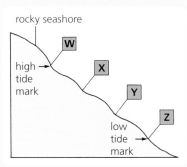

type of periwinkle	location			
	W	X	Y	Z
rough	2	3	1	0
small	4	2	0	0
flat	0	1	4	2

Table 19.1

Figure 19.6

From these data it can be concluded that
A rough periwinkles are most numerous near the low tide mark.
B small periwinkles are most numerous near the low tide mark.
C flat periwinkles are adapted to survive long periods out of water.
D small periwinkles are adapted to survive long periods out of water.

Questions 7 and 8 refer to Figure 19.7.

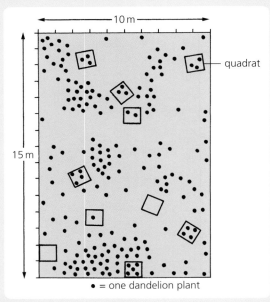

Figure 19.7

7   Based only on the information given in Figure 19.7, an accurate estimate of the total number of dandelion plants growing on the lawn would be

A   2.5   B   25.0   C   37.5   D   375.0

8   The reliability of the estimate could be improved by

A   setting up a control experiment.   B   taking a larger number of quadrat samples.

C   spraying the lawn with weedkiller.   D   repeating the survey on a neighbour's lawn of the same size.

Questions 9 and 10 refer to the following information.

During an investigation, five soil samples (each 1 m^2 x 0.1 m) were taken once per month from a field and the number of earthworms present in each counted. Soil surface temperatures were also measured. Mean values were calculated for both sets of results and used to plot the graph shown in Figure 19.8.

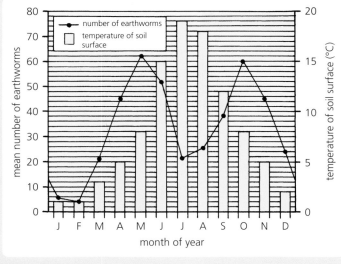

Figure 19.8

9 Which 2 months of the year were found to share the same values for mean number of earthworms and soil surface temperature?

    A January and February

    B March and December

    C May and October

    D April and November

10 The earthworms were most abundant at soil surface temperatures (in °C) of

    A 8   **B** 16   **C** 19   **D** 32

11 Figure 19.9 shows four tubes set up to measure the pH of soil. Which one is correct?

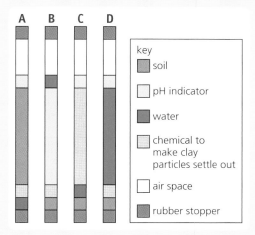

Figure 19.9

12 During an investigation into the effect of light intensity on the distribution of bluebell plants in a wood, the meter shown in Figure 19.10 was used to take readings at quadrats 1–10 where the abundance level of bluebell plants was also measured.

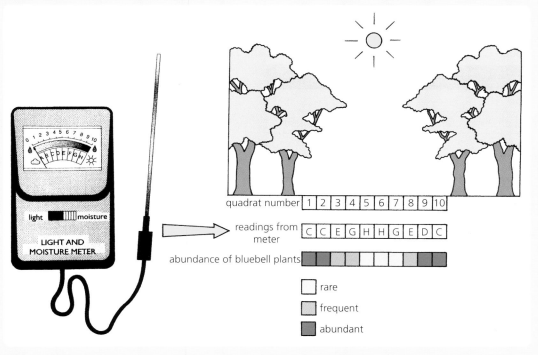

Figure 19.10

From this survey, it can be concluded that bluebell plants grow better in

A dimly lit conditions than in brightly lit conditions.

B moist conditions than in dry conditions.

C brightly lit conditions than in dimly lit conditions.

D dry conditions than in moist conditions.

13 Table 19.2 describes some of the features of six types of bird. These can be identified using the key of paired statements below the table. However the key is incomplete.

bird	colour of wings	legs	number of eggs laid	tail length	tail shape
black grouse	blue–black with white bar	feathered	6–10	short	fan-shaped
capercailie	brown	feathered	5–8	short	fan-shaped
partridge	brown	scaly	12–18	short	not fan-shaped
pheasant	brown	scaly	8–15	long	not fan-shaped
ptarmigan	white	feathered	5–9	short	not fan-shaped
red grouse	brown	feathered	4–9	short	not fan-shaped

Table 19.2

1 wings brown .... go to 2

   wings not brown .... go to 5

2 legs feathered .... go to 3

   legs scaly .... go to 4

3 tail fan-shaped .... Capercailie

   tail not fan-shaped .... Red grouse

4 _____ X _____ .... Pheasant

   _____ Y _____ .... Partridge

5 wings blue-black with white bar..................................... Black grouse

   wings white... Ptarmigan

   Which row in Table 19.3 gives the correct answers to blanks X and Y in the key?

	blank X	blank Y
A	tail short	tail long
B	fewer than 7 eggs laid	more than 7 eggs laid
C	tail long	tail short
D	more than 7 eggs laid	fewer than 7 eggs laid

Table 19.3

14 Figure 19.11 shows three animals P, Q and R caught using tree-beating as a sampling technique to investigate an ecosystem. (They are not drawn to scale.) The diagram is followed by a key.

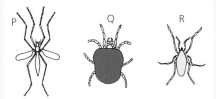

Figure 19.11

1 Animal has three pairs of legs .... go to 2
  Animal has four pairs of legs .... go to 4
2 Body is green .... greenfly
  Body is not green .... go to 3
3 Body is round and spotted .... ladybird
  Body is not round and spotted .... crane fly
4 Body is in one part .... go to 5
  Body is in two parts .... spider
5 Legs are longer than the body .... harvestman
  Legs are shorter than the body .... mite

Use the key to establish which row in Table 19.4 correctly identifies animals P, Q and R.

	P	Q	R
A	harvestman	mite	crane fly
B	crane fly	mite	harvestman
C	harvestman	ladybird	crane fly
D	crane fly	ladybird	harvestman

Table 19.4

15 The graph in Figure 19.12 shows the range of dissolved oxygen concentration within which each of six species of freshwater animal is found to occur. Which species would be found at the following two concentrations of dissolved oxygen?

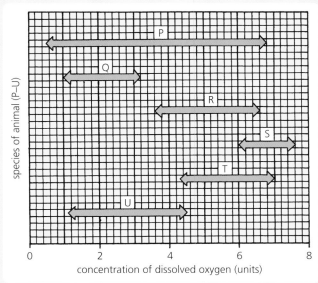

	concentration of dissolved oxygen (units)	
	3.4	6.9
A	P and U only	P, S and T
B	P, Q and U	S and T only
C	P and U only	S and T only
D	P, Q and U	P, S and T

Table 19.5

Figure 19.12

16 An investigation into the effect of increasing salt concentration on percentage seed germination was carried out using seeds from four species of plant (W, X, Y and Z) native to mud flats at a river estuary. The graph in Figure 19.13 shows the results.

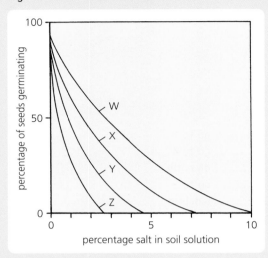

Figure 19.13

Which row in Table 19.6 gives the correct answers to the blanks in the following conclusions drawn from these results? As the percentage of salt in the soil decreases, the percentage of seeds that germinate ___1___, with percentage salt in soil solution acting as ___2___ factor. Species ___3___ is most likely to have seeds able to germinate nearest to the sea.

	blank 1	blank 2	blank 3
A	increases	an abiotic	W
B	decreases	a biotic	W
C	increases	a biotic	Z
D	decreases	an abiotic	Z

Table 19.6

17 Table 19.7 gives the results of a survey on the species of fish in a river.

sampling point of river	pH of water at sampling point	species of fish found at sampling point								distance of sampling point from sea (km)
		P	Q	R	S	T	U	V	W	
1	8.85	✔	✔	✔	✔	✔	✔	✘	✔	90
2	8.82	✘	✘	✔	✔	✔	✔	✔	✔	80
3	8.21	✘	✘	✘	✔	✔	✘	✔	✔	70
4	8.00	✘	✘	✘	✘	✔	✔	✔	✔	60
5	7.60	✘	✘	✘	✘	✘	✔	✔	✔	50
6	7.48	✘	✘	✘	✘	✘	✘	✔	✔	40
7	7.24	✘	✘	✘	✘	✘	✘	✘	✔	30

Table 19.7

(✔ = present, ✘ = absent)

The number of different species found at pH values of less than 8.00 was

A 3   B 4   C 6   D 10

Questions 18, 19 and 20 refer to Figure 19.14. It shows the results of a survey of five types of seaweed. Quadrats were placed every 2 metres in a line transect down the rocky shore from the high tide mark to the low tide mark. Each type of seaweed was given an abundance score (see key).

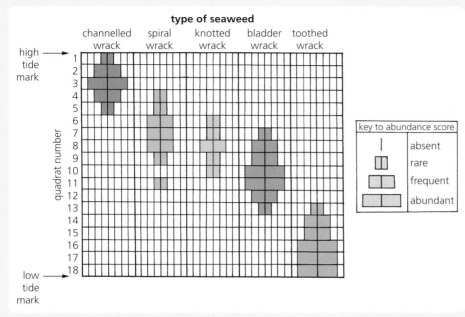

Figure 19.14

18 How many types of wrack showed an abundance score of frequent in two of the quadrats in which the wrack occurred?

   A 1   **B** 2   **C** 3   **D** 4

19 How many quadrats contained more than two types of wrack?

   A 3   **B** 4   **C** 5   **D** 8

20 Which type of wrack would be exposed to air for the LEAST time during every 24-hour period?

   A channelled   **B** spiral   **C** bladder   **D** toothed

20 Adaptation, natural selection and evolution

Matching test

Match the terms in list X with their descriptions in list Y.

list X
1) adaptation
2) antibiotic-resistant
3) evolution
4) isolating mechanism
5) mutagenic
6) mutation
7) natural selection
8) selection pressure
9) selective advantage
10) speciation
11) species
12) variation

list Y
a) process by which individuals best adapted to the environment survive and pass their genes on to succeeding generations
b) process involving natural selection that has transformed life on Earth from its earliest beginnings to its present diverse state
c) term describing an agent which increases the mutation rate
d) differences due to inherited (and environmental) factors that exist between the members of a species
e) force of natural selection acting on the diverse members of a species to the advantage of some but not others
f) group of genetically similar organisms that produce fertile offspring and share the same basic anatomy and physiology
g) formation of new species
h) barrier which prevents gene exchange between sub-populations of a species
i) benefit gained by mutant organisms in an environment which suits them but not other members of the population
j) type of microorganism whose growth is not inhibited by chemicals such as penicillin
k) random change in the structure or composition of an organism's genetic material
l) inherited characteristic that makes an organism well suited to its environment and increases its chance of survival

Multiple choice test

Choose the ONE correct answer to each of the following multiple choice questions.

1 Which of the following statements is NOT correct?
  A Under natural conditions, mutations arise spontaneously and at random.
  B Mutations may be neutral or may confer an advantage or a disadvantage.
  C Certain environmental factors can increase the rate of mutation artificially.
  D Mutations are one of many sources of new alleles upon which natural selection can act.

2 The mutation frequency of a gene is expressed as the number of mutations that occur at that gene site per million gametes. If the chance of the mutant allele for albino coat in mice arising is 1 in 100 000, then the mutation frequency of this allele per million gametes is
  A 10   B 100   C 1000   D 10 000

3 Ebony-coloured body is a mutant characteristic caused by an allele whose mutation frequency is 20 per million gametes. The chance of a new mutation occurring is therefore
  A 1 in 500   B 1 in 5000   C 1 in 50 000   D 1 in 500 000

4 Which of the following does NOT act as a mutagenic agent?
  A high temperatures
  B X-rays
  C low temperatures
  D mustard gas

5 The graph in Figure 20.1 shows the effect of increasing radiation on the number of barley grains that germinate out of a total of 300 used at each treatment.

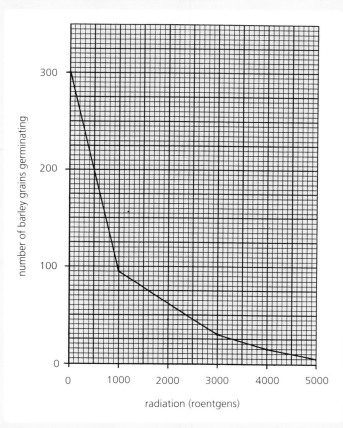

Figure 20.1

What percentage decrease in number of seeds germinating occurred between 0 and 4000 roentgens?

A 15   B 95   C 98   D 285

6 Table 20.1 shows the results from an investigation into the effect of increased dosage of radiation on the percentage number of shoots from germinating seeds that develop abnormal leaves.

radiation (roentgens)	percentage of shoots with abnormal leaves
0	0
1000	10
2000	20
3000	30
4000	50
5000	100

Table 20.1

Which of the graphs in Figure 20.2 correctly represents these results?

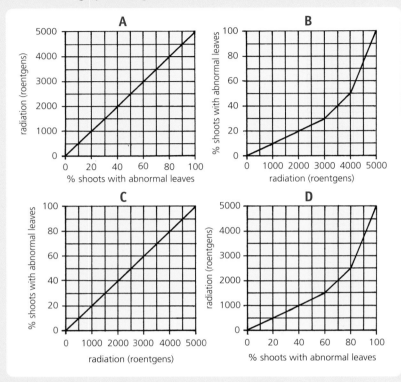

Figure 20.2

7 Which of the following is an example of a behavioural adaptation that helps the kangaroo rat to survive in the desert?
  A It does not produce any sweat.
  B It remains in its burrow during the day.
  C Its kidneys make extremely concentrated urine.
  D Its large intestine is highly efficient at reabsorbing water from waste.
8 Figure 20.3 shows a cactus plant.

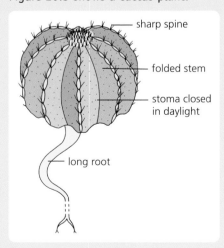

Figure 20.3

Which of the following is NOT a structural adaptation that promotes its survival in the desert?
  A leaves reduced to spines to deter attack by thirsty animals
  B stem folded allowing expansion and contraction subject to water availability
  C roots extremely long to enable them to reach subterranean water
  D stomatal rhythm reversed so that stomata close in daylight and open in darkness

9 Which of the following is a behavioural adaptation?
  A the strong, hard shell of a barnacle that resists damage by wave action
  B the decrease in rate of activity of a blowfly larva that it shows in dark conditions
  C the yellow pigments in a shade plant's leaves that help it to photosynthesise in dim light
  D the strong holdfast of a brown seaweed that attaches it firmly to submerged rocks

10 Table 20.2 shows the reproductive potential of some animal species.

animal species	mean number of offspring per year
fox	5
red grouse	8
rabbit	24
mouse	30
trout	800
cod	4 000 000
oyster	16 000 000

Table 20.2

Compared to red grouse, the reproductive potential of cod is greater by a factor of
  A 50 000 times   B 500 000 times   C 3 200 000 times   D 32 000 000 times

11 Which of the following does NOT form part of the theory of evolution proposed by Charles Darwin?
  A Any beneficial change in an organism's phenotype is brought about by the direct action of the environment.
  B Members of the same species are not identical but show variation in all characteristics.
  C A struggle for existence occurs because organisms tend to produce more offspring than the environment will support.
  D Those offspring whose phenotypes are less well suited to the environment are more likely to die before producing offspring.

Questions 12, 13, 14, and 15 refer to the following information.

The peppered moth exists in two forms: the light-coloured wild-type variety and the less common dark (melanic) type. In an experiment, individuals of both types were marked on their underside with a dot of paint and then some were released in a rural area and some were released in an industrial area polluted with smoke and soot. Many of these marked moths were later recaptured as shown in Table 20.3.

	rural area		industrial area	
	light moth	melanic moth	light moth	melanic moth
number of marked moths released	250	200	250	300
number of marked moths recaptured	40	see question 13	45	162
percentage number of marked moths recaptured	16	4	18	54

Table 20.3

12 Melanic moths occur as a result of
  A industrial pollution.   B natural selection.   C evolution.   D mutation.
13 How many melanic moths were recaptured in the rural area?
  A 2   B 4   C 8   D 20

14 From the data in the table, it is NOT valid to conclude that
   A in the rural area, light moths were four times more likely to survive than melanic moths.
   B a greater percentage of both types of moth were recaptured in the industrial area compared with the rural area.
   C in the industrial area, melanic moths were three times more likely to survive than light-coloured moths.
   D the total percentage number of light moths recaptured in both areas exceeded the total percentage number of melanic moths recaptured.

15 The melanic moth enjoys a selective advantage in an industrial area because
   A predators fail to notice it against a sooty background.
   B there is no competition since the light form is killed by pollution.
   C predators ignore it because it is dirty and noxious to eat.
   D it is easily seen against light-coloured tree trunks.

16 The 'high speed' evolution of bacterial population 1 into bacterial population 2 is shown in Figure 20.4.

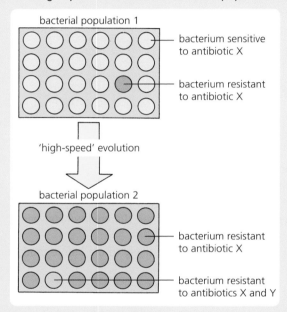

Figure 20.4

This form of evolution would involve THREE of the processes given in list Q. These are
A 1, 3 and 6   B 1, 4 and 5   C 2, 3 and 5   D 2, 4 and 6
list Q
   1 application of antibiotic X to population 1
   2 application of antibiotic Y to population 2
   3 multiplication of surviving bacterium resistant to antibiotic X
   4 multiplication of surviving bacterium resistant to antibiotic Y
   5 mutation producing bacterium resistant to antibiotic X
   6 mutation producing bacterium resistant to antibiotic Y

17 Which of the following is NOT an example of natural selection in action?
   A emergence of rats which thrive on warfarin rat poison
   B development of pedigree strains of Rottweiler dogs
   C resistance of certain types of bacteria to penicillin
   D survival of cotton bollworm moths treated with insecticide

18 Which of the following statements is FALSE?
   The use of antibiotics in the feed of farm animals
   A   prevents bacterial growth and promotes weight increase in farm animals.
   B   produces strains of farm animals genetically resistant to disease.
   C   leads to the selection of bacteria resistant to antibiotics.
   D   increases the risk of resistant pathogens affecting humans.

19 Members of the same species
   A   are unable to produce fertile offspring.
   B   are genetically isolated from one another.
   C   possess the same complement of chromosomes.
   D   can successfully interbreed with members of other species.

20 Which of the following occurs during the process of speciation?
   A   formation of new species from existing ones
   B   mass extinction of several species in a disturbed environment
   C   alteration in a species' phenotype caused by environmental change
   D   production of sterile offspring by interbreeding between two different species

21 Three of the events that occur during speciation are
   1   mutation
   2   natural selection
   3   isolation
   The correct order in which these occur is
   A   3, 2, 1   B   2, 1, 3   C   3, 1, 2   D   2, 3, 1

22 Which of the following does NOT act as an ecological barrier during speciation?
   A   low temperature
   B   high humidity
   C   acidic pH
   D   mating behaviour

23 Areas X, Y and Z in Figure 20.5 represent three populations of a species of a grassland-dwelling animal which is
   unable to fly or swim.

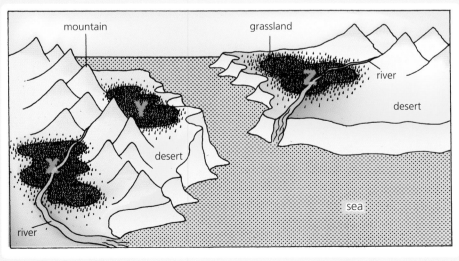

Figure 20.5

The barriers preventing interbreeding between populations X and Y and Y and Z respectively are

A desert and sea.

B mountains and river.

C desert and river.

D mountains and sea.

24 Which of the following factors can impose a selection pressure on a sub-population during the process of speciation?

A change in climate

B variation in genotype

C well adapted phenotype

D increased rate of mutation

25 *Sorbus arranensis* is a slender tree native to the island of Arran. Such a species that occurs only within a localised area is said to be

A biotic to the area.

B abiotic to the area.

C endemic to the area.

D mutagenic to the area.

21 Human impact on the environment

Matching test
Match the terms in list X with their descriptions in list Y.

list X
1) algal bloom
2) bioaccumulation
3) biological control
4) fertiliser
5) genetically modified (GM) crop
6) indicator species
7) intensive farming
8) leaching
9) lichen
10) monoculture
11) pesticide
12) pollution
13) sulphur dioxide

list Y
a) substance rich in chemicals such as nitrate essential for healthy plant growth
b) loss of soluble chemicals from soil solution to a local waterway in rainwater run-off
c) result of rapid growth of populations of simple water plants
d) organisms whose presence shows the state of an environment's health
e) contamination of an environment by harmful substances
f) general name for chemical used to kill pest species
g) increase in concentration of a non-biodegradable chemical (such as DDT) in the cells of the organisms along a food chain
h) simple plant which indicates the level of air pollution by sulphur dioxide gas
i) reduction of a pest population by the deliberate introduction of one of its natural enemies
j) poisonous gas that harms living things and reduces biodiversity
k) domesticated plant that has been altered by genetic engineering to give greater food yield or resistance to pests
l) vast cultivated population of one type of crop plant whose members are often genetically identical
m) form of agriculture which gives increased yield by growing crop monocultures and by 'battery-farming' animals

Multiple choice test
Choose the ONE correct answer to each of the following multiple choice questions.

1 Which row in Table 21.1 is NOT correct?

	intensive-farming practice	possible disadvantage
A	cultivation of vast monocultures of high-yielding crop plants	large quantities of chemical fertiliser needed
B	use of herbicide to remove weeds from crop area	increase in biodiversity of wild plants and animals
C	rearing of farm animals indoors in restricted spaces	increased risk of animals suffering from disease and stress
D	use of insecticides to remove insects that feed on crops	helpful insects may be poisoned

Table 21.1

➜

2 The data in Table 21.2 show the effect of adding nitrate fertiliser on the yield of grain from a cereal crop.

concentration of nitrate fertiliser (kg/ha)	grain yield (kg/ha)
0	1000
50	3000
100	3400
150	3700
200	4800
250	4800
300	4400
350	4700
400	5000

Table 21.2

Which of the graphs in Figure 21.1 correctly presents these results as a line of best fit?

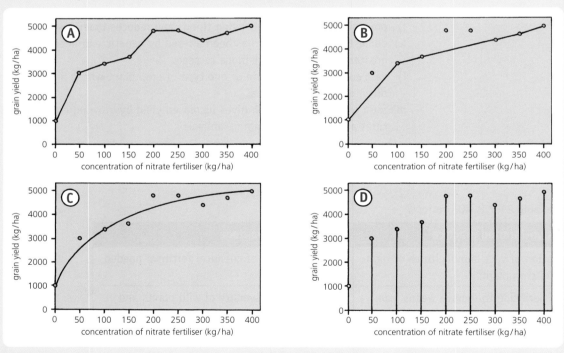

Figure 21.1

Questions 3 and 4 refer to the graph in Figure 21.2. It shows the results of an investigation into the effect on a crop of applying fertiliser containing different concentrations of nitrate and phosphate.

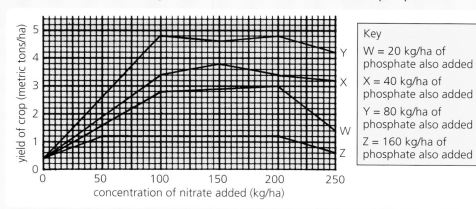

Key

W = 20 kg/ha of phosphate also added

X = 40 kg/ha of phosphate also added

Y = 80 kg/ha of phosphate also added

Z = 160 kg/ha of phosphate also added

Figure 21.2

3 The lowest concentrations (in kg/ha) of nitrate and phosphate that gave optimum crop yield were

	nitrate	phosphate
A	100	80
B	150	40
C	200	80
D	250	40

Table 21.3

4 Compared with yield at 200 kg/ha of nitrate + 80 kg/ha of phosphate, the yield at 200 kg/ha of nitrate + 160 kg/ha of phosphate shows a percentage decrease of

A 12   B 36   C 48   D 75

5 The boxes in Figure 21.3 give the events leading to and following the formation of an algal bloom in a loch. They are in the wrong order.

① Dead plants and algae are decomposed by aerobic bacteria.

② Algae grow rapidly forming a bloom.

③ Bacterial growth depletes the loch water's oxygen supply.

④ Fertiliser containing nitrate leaches into loch water.

⑤ Submerged aquatic plants are deprived of light and die.

Figure 21.3

The correct order of these events is

A 2, 4, 5, 1, 3   B 4, 2, 3, 1, 5   C 2, 4, 5, 3, 1   D 4, 2, 5, 1, 3

6   The graph in Figure 21.4 shows the progress of an algal bloom in a river following the run-off of fertiliser rich in nitrate from nearby fields in rainwater. Which row in Table 21.4 gives the correct identities of W, X and Y?

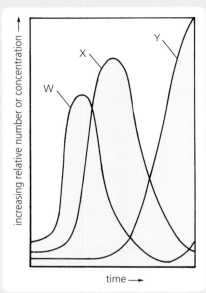

	relative number of algae	relative number of bacteria	relative concentration of nitrate
A	Y	X	W
B	X	W	Y
C	W	Y	X
D	X	Y	W

Table 21.4

Figure 21.4

7   To reduce the chance of nitrate being leached out of the soil, the farmer should apply fertiliser
   A   when the cereal crop is actively growing.
   B   when the soil is bare and fallow in winter.
   C   in the early autumn before the ground freezes over.
   D   in one large dose rather than several smaller ones.

8   Figure 21.5 shows a simplified version of the nitrogen cycle.

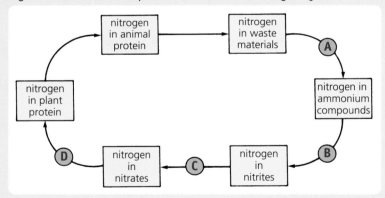

Figure 21.5

Effluent from adequately treated sewage when discharged into a river may lead to an algal bloom. Which arrow in Figure 21.5 represents the stage in the cycle at which this growth would occur?

9 Table 21.5 summarises the results from an investigation into the impact of a new pesticide on four pests.

crop	pest	mean loss of crop (acres/year)	
		with pesticide	without pesticide
potato	leatherjacket	1750	1800
cabbage	caterpillar	350	3100
apple	aphid	550	11500
pea	weevil	450	4500

Table 21.5

On which pest was the pesticide most effective?

A leatherjacket   B caterpillar   C aphid   D weevil

Questions 10 and 11 refer to Figure 21.6. It shows the members of a food chain and, in brackets, the concentration in parts per million (ppm) of a non-biodegradable pesticide residue in their tissues. The water in their ecosystem contains 0.00005 ppm of pesticide.

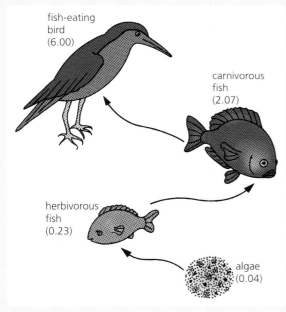

fish-eating bird (6.00)

carnivorous fish (2.07)

herbivorous fish (0.23)

algae (0.04)

Figure 21.6

10 The original source of energy for this food chain was
   A sunlight.   B pond water.   C algae.   D a fish-eating bird.
11 The concentration of pesticide increased by a factor of nine times between
   A water and algae.
   B algae and herbivorous fish.
   C herbivorous fish and carnivorous fish.
   D carnivorous fish and fish-eating bird.

12 Table 21.6 shows the results of spraying four new pesticides on to sample areas of a particular crop which was later harvested and used as animal feed. Which pesticide is BOTH safe and effective?

pesticide	mean loss of crop (acres/year)		effect of feeding sprayed crop to pregnant cattle
	without pesticide	with pesticide	
A	10 000	10 000	heavier calves develop
B	8 000	10 000	more offspring produced
C	15 000	1 000	smaller calves develop
D	12 000	1 000	normal offspring produced

Table 21.6

Questions 13 and 14 refer to the following information.

The Dayak people of Borneo live in long houses raised on stilts. Each house is really a village under one roof. The people's diet consists mainly of rice, fish and wild game. Many years ago, the World Health Organisation (WHO) attempted to reduce the incidence of malaria amongst the Dayak people by spraying the long houses with DDT to kill mosquitoes. The campaign against malaria was successful but DDT was also absorbed by cockroaches that lived in the long houses. These were consumed by lizards that were eaten by cats. The cats died and failed to keep the number of rats down. The rats carried fleas which bit the people giving them a form of plague.

Figure 21.7 shows a simplified version of the food web present in the long-house ecosystem.

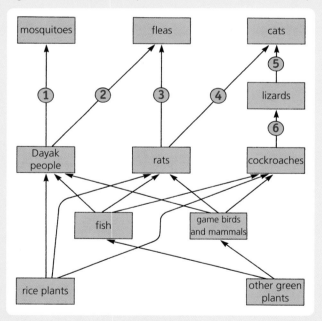

Figure 21.7

13 Which numbered arrows in the food web ALL eventually broke down as a result of DDT disturbing this delicate ecosystem?

   A 1, 3 and 5   B 1, 4 and 5   C 2, 3 and 6   D 2, 4 and 6

14 With reference only to the information given in the passage, which numbered links represent the flow of energy in one direction and the transmission of disease in the opposite direction?

   A 1 and 2   B 2 and 3   C 1 and 4   D 3 and 6

Questions 15 and 16 refer to Figure 21.8. It charts the oxygen concentration of the water in a river from where it meets the sea back to its source 44 miles inland. This river has suffered pollution by untreated sewage.

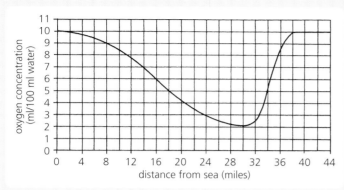

Figure 21.8

15 The distance from the sea, in miles, at which the organic effluent was added was

  A 2   **B** 30   **C** 38   **D** 44

16 Stonefly nymphs are adapted to life in oxygen concentrations of more than 3 ml per 100 ml of water. The distance from the sea, in miles, at which stonefly nymphs would be found is

  A 22   **B** 26   **C** 28   **D** 32

Questions 17 and 18 refer to the graph in Figure 21.9. It shows the results from a survey done on the number of lichen species growing along a 20-km transect, from the centre of a city out to a country area.

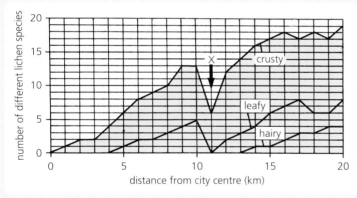

Figure 21.9

17 The dip in the graph at arrow X indicates

  A an area of especially clean air.

  B an area lacking both hairy and crusty lichens.

  C a local increase in sulphur dioxide concentration of air.

  D a lower level of atmospheric pollution compared with the country area.

18 Twenty-eight different species of lichen were recorded at one of the sites. The distance (in km) of this site from the city centre was

  A 16   **B** 17   **C** 18   **D** 19

Questions 19 and 20 refer to Table 21.7. It shows the effect that the state of the water in a river had on the abundance of three types of river organism.

		state of river water				
		very clean	clean	fairly clean	dirty	very dirty
relative abundance of river organism studied	green algae	scarce	moderate	plentiful	abundant	abundant
	trout	plentiful	scarce	usually nil	see question 20	nil
	water weeds	scarce	plentiful	see question 19	plentiful	scarce

Table 21.7

19 In fairly clean water, the relative abundance of water weeds would have been

  A nil.   B plentiful.   C moderate.   D scarce.

20 In dirty water, the relative abundance of the trout population would have been

  A nil.   B scarce.   C moderate.   D plentiful.

Questions 21 and 22 refer to the stacked bar chart in Figure 21.10. It shows the results of a survey on the damage caused by atmospheric pollution to trees in a forest in a northern European country.

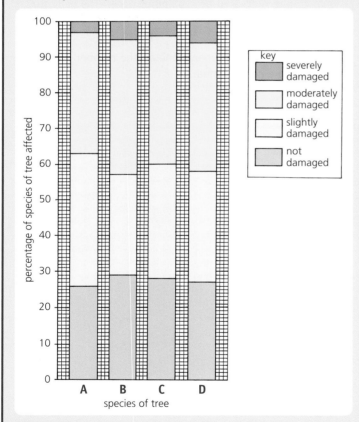

Figure 21.10

21 Thirty four per cent of the population of one of the species of tree suffered moderate damage. Which species of tree?

22 Which of the species shows a ratio of no damage:slight:moderate:severe of 7:8:9:1?

23 For successful biological control of red spider mites (M) on cucumber plants in a greenhouse, a supplier of *Phytoseiulus* (P), their predator, recommends the use of 200 P to deal with a population of 6000 M. How many P should be ordered to deal with a population of 36 000 M?

    A 600   **B** 1200   **C** 1800   **D** 12 000

Questions 24 and 25 refer to the graph in Figure 21.11. It shows the results of using *Phytoseiulus* as the predator to control whitefly on cucumber plants in a glasshouse. The infested plants were divided into two groups, X and Y. Predators were released onto the plants in group Y at week 4. Group X received no predators.

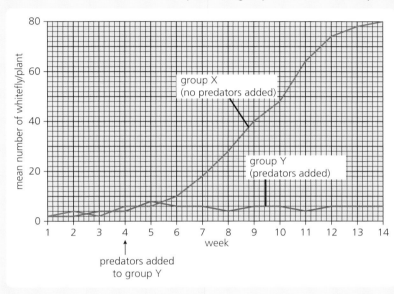

Figure 21.11

24 By how many times was the number of whitefly per plant greater on the untreated plants compared with the plants treated with the predator at week 11?

    A 4   **B** 16   **C** 64   **D** 256

25 What percentage increase in the mean number of whitefly per plant occurred between week 5 and week 13 in the absence of predators?

    A 72   **B** 78   **C** 875   **D** 1200

Specimen Examination 1

Choose the ONE correct answer to each of the following multiple choice questions.

1 Figure 1 shows a cell from a green plant.

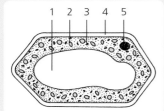

Figure 1

Which of the following structures would ALL be ABSENT from an animal cell?

A 1, 2 and 4   B 1, 2 and 5   C 2, 3 and 4   D 2, 3 and 5

2 The tissue fluid that bathes living cells in the human body is equal in water concentration to 0.85% salt solution. If human pancreatic cells were immersed in 5% salt solution, they would

A lose water by osmosis and shrink.   B lose water by active transport and shrink.

C gain water by osmosis and burst.   D gain water by active transport and burst.

3 Figure 2 shows a typical S-shaped growth curve. Which region of the graph represents the period of decelerating growth?

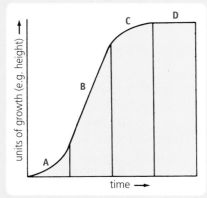

Figure 2

4 Which of the flow charts in Figure 3 correctly shows the route taken by the genetic information involved in the production of a protein in a cell?

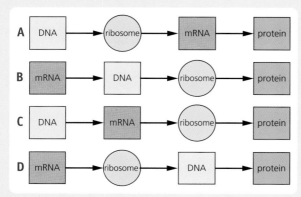

Figure 3

5   Which of the graphs in Figure 4 shows the effect of temperature on the activity of an enzyme from the human body?

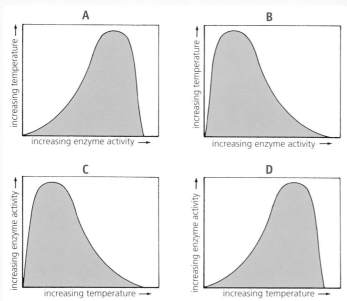

Figure 4

6   Figure 5 shows the release, during respiration in aerobic conditions, of the energy needed to synthesise protein. Which box represents the correct position of ATP in this scheme?

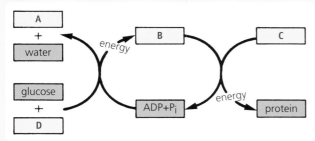

Figure 5

7   If an animal of mass 100 g consumes 50 cm³ of oxygen in 30 minutes, then its respiratory rate in cm³ of oxygen used per gram of body tissue per hour is
    A   0.25   B   0.50   C   1.00   D   2.00

8   A variegated leaf on a destarched ivy plant was treated as shown in Figure 6.

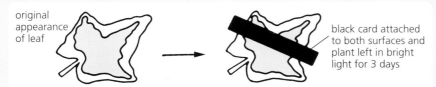

Figure 6

Which part of Figure 7 shows the appearance of the leaf after testing it for starch?

Figure 7

9 During growth at a root tip, a cell undergoes the following processes:
  1 specialisation
  2 division
  3 elongation
  These occur in the order
  A 2, 1, 3   **B** 1, 2, 3   **C** 1, 3, 2   **D** 2, 3, 1

10 Figure 8 shows a simplified version of the means by which the blood sugar level is controlled in the human body.

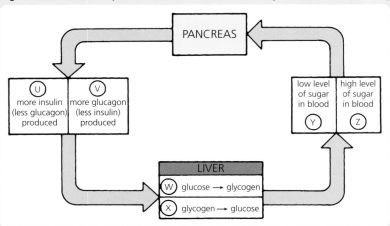

Figure 8

Which of the following responses would occur in the human body as a direct result of fasting for 24 hours?
  A Y, V, X   **B** Z, U, W   **C** Y, U, X   **D** Z, V, W

11 Figure 9 represents the human life cycle. Which row in Table 1 correctly identifies the processes represented by the numbered boxes in the diagram?

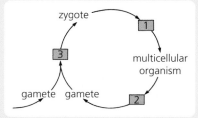

Figure 9

Table 1

	1	2	3
A	mitosis	fertilisation	gamete production
B	gamete production	mitosis	fertilisation
C	fertilisation	gamete production	mitosis
D	mitosis	gamete production	fertilisation

12 Various crosses involving three red-flowering plants (1, 2 and 3) and one white-flowering plant (4) were carried out as shown in Table 2.

cross	offspring produced	
	red-flowering (%)	white-flowering (%)
1 x 4	100	0
2 x 4	50	50
2 x 3	75	25

Table 2

Which of the following plants have the same genotype?

A 1 and 2   **B** 1 and 3   **C** 2 and 3   **D** 1, 2 and 3

13 Transpiration is the
A loss of water through the leaves of a plant.
B movement of mineral salts up a plant's stem.
C transport of sugar down to the roots of a plant.
D passage of water through a plant's xylem vessels.

14 Which of the following is NOT one of the features typical of alveoli that makes their structure perfectly suited to their function of gas exchange?
A very thin wall
B rings of cartilage
C large surface area
D extensive blood supply

15 The data in Table 3 show the effect of cigarette smoking on the life expectancy of British men.

present age (years)	further years expected to live (life expectancy)			
	non-smoker	1–10 cigarettes daily	11–20 cigarettes daily	21+ cigarettes daily
25	49	44	43	42
35	39	35	34	33
45	30	26	25	24
55	21	18	17	16

Table 3

Compared with non-smokers, the number of years by which 45-year-old men who smoke 21+ cigarettes daily reduce their life expectancy is

A 5   **B** 6   **C** 21   **D** 24

16 Which row in Table 4 gives the correct answers to the blanks in the following sentence?
An ecosystem consists of all the organisms (the ___1___), each organism living in a particular place (its ___2___), and the non-living (___3___) components with which the organisms interact.

	blank 1	blank 2	blank 3
A	community	habitat	abiotic
B	population	niche	abiotic
C	community	niche	biotic
D	population	habitat	biotic

Table 4

17 Figure 10 shows a woodland food web.

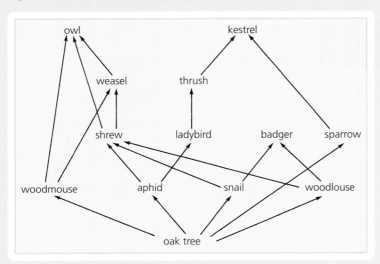

Figure 10

Figure 11 shows four pyramids of numbers extracted from the food web. Which one is correct?

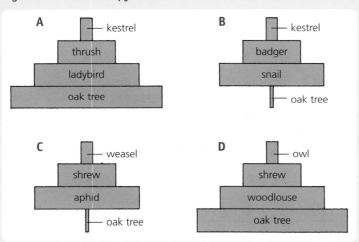

Figure 11

18 The graph in Figure 12 shows the effect of crowding on the birth rate in water fleas.

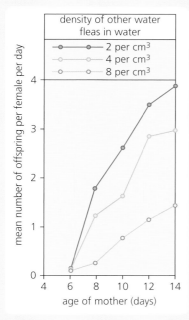

Figure 12

Which row in Table 5 gives the correct answers to the blanks in the following paragraph?
The number of offspring produced per female per day __1__ as population density of other water fleas in the sur-rounding water __2__. In this case, population density is acting as __3__ factor.

	blank 1	blank 2	blank 3
A	decreases	decreases	an abiotic
B	increases	decreases	an abiotic
C	increases	increases	a biotic
D	decreases	increases	a biotic

Table 5

19 Which of the following is an example of a desert animal exhibiting a behavioural adaptation?
   A the rattlesnake which possesses a scaly, waterproof body covering
   B the lizard which spends time in the shade to lower its body temperature
   C the kangaroo rat which has kidneys able to make very concentrated urine
   D the camel which has long thick eye lashes for protection during sand storms
20 Excess fertiliser from farmland can damage a nearby waterway by
   A poisoning the fish that consume it.
   B being toxic to submerged aquatic plants.
   C depriving submerged aquatic plants of carbon dioxide for photosynthesis.
   D causing an algal bloom that leads to lack of oxygen in the water.

Specimen Examination 2

Choose the ONE correct answer to each of the following multiple choice questions.

1 Figure 1 shows *Euglena viridis*, a unicellular organism that lives in pond water.

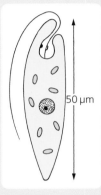

50 µm

Figure 1

Which of the following expresses the organism's length as a decimal fraction of a millimetre (mm)?

A 0.5   B 0.05   C 0.005   D 0.0005

2 Diffusion is important to the unicellular animal *Amoeba* because it is the means by which

A CO_2, a waste product, enters and oxygen, a useful substance, leaves.

B oxygen, a waste product, enters and CO_2, a useful substance, leaves.

C CO_2, a useful substance, enters and oxygen, a waste product, leaves.

D oxygen, a useful substance, enters and CO_2, a waste product, leaves.

3 The experiment shown in Figure 2 was set up to investigate the action of live yeast cells on glucose in the absence of oxygen.

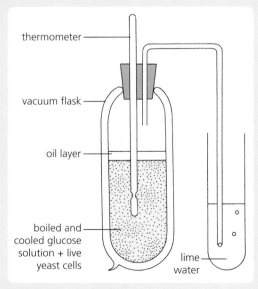

thermometer

vacuum flask

oil layer

boiled and cooled glucose solution + live yeast cells

lime water

Figure 2

A control experiment should also have been set up where the

A oil was replaced by alcohol.

B glucose was replaced by fresh fruit juice.

C live yeast was replaced by dead yeast.

D lime water was replaced by a hydrogen carbonate indicator.

4   Which of boxes A–D in Figure 3 contains the mRNA strand that is complementary to the DNA strand in box Y?

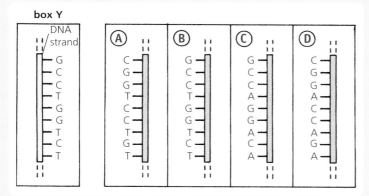

Figure 3

5   Albumin is a protein found in egg white. A protease is a protein-digesting enzyme. To investigate the effect of pH on the activity of two proteases, X and Y, on albumin, the experiment shown in Figure 4 was carried out.

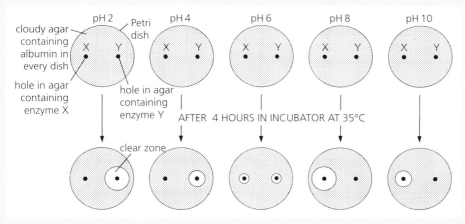

Figure 4

At which pH were the enzymes equally active?

A   2   B   4   C   6   D   8

6 Figure 5 shows eight of the stages involved in the process of genetic engineering. What is their correct sequence?

A Q, T, S, U, W, P, R, V

B T, Q, P, U, W, S, R, V

C Q, T, P, U, S, W, V, R

D T, Q, U, P, S, W, R, V

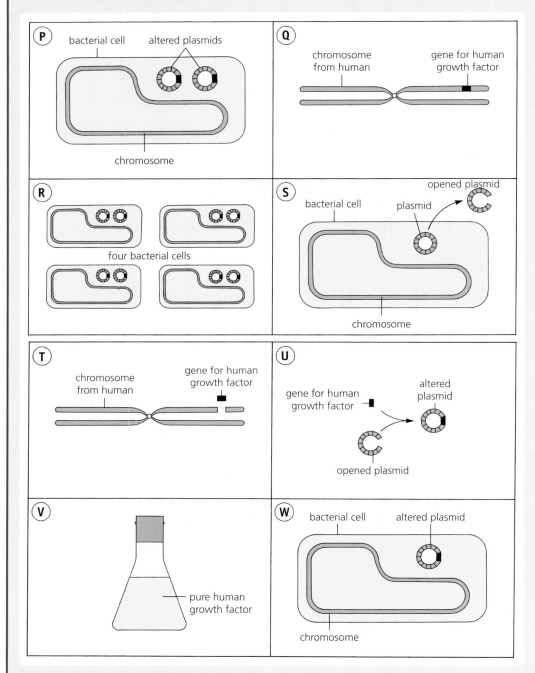

Figure 5

7 Which of the following substances is required by a yeast cell for fermentation?

A water   B glucose   C ethanol   D lactic acid

8 Which of the following substances are BOTH raw materials used in the process of photosynthesis?

A water and oxygen   B oxygen and glucose

C glucose and carbon dioxide   D carbon dioxide and water

9 Which row in Table 1 correctly describes stem cells?

	source of cells	state of cells
A	animal	specialised
B	bacteria	specialised
C	animal	non-specialised
D	bacteria	non-specialised

Table 1

10 Which part of Figure 6 shows the correct sequence of neurons in a reflex arc?

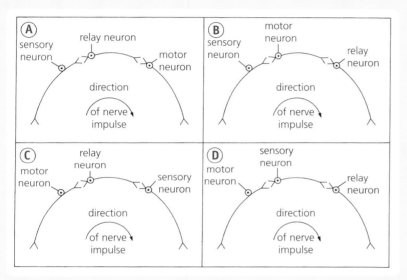

Figure 6

11 Which column in Table 2 describes a reflex action?

	A	B	C	D
rapid	✔	✘	✔	✔
slow	✘	✔	✘	✘
protective	✔	✔	✔	✘
non-protective	✘	✘	✘	✔
voluntary	✘	✘	✔	✘
involuntary	✔	✔	✘	✔

Table 2

12 In a human female, fertilisation normally takes place in the
   A vagina.   B uterus.   C oviduct.   D ovary.

13 In guinea pigs, long hair is recessive to short hair. If a large group of long-haired females is crossed with a large group of heterozygous males, the percentage of their offspring that are long-haired will be approximately
   A 25   B 50   C 75   D 100

14 Figure 7 shows the rates of water absorption and transpiration that occurred in a sunflower plant during a 24-hour period.

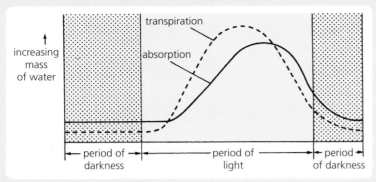

Figure 7

From this evidence, it is true to say that in
A   light, absorption rate always exceeds transpiration rate.
B   dark, transpiration rate always exceeds absorption rate.
C   light, transpiration rate always exceeds absorption rate.
D   dark, absorption rate always exceeds transpiration rate.

15 Which row in Table 3 correctly refers to peristalsis?

	state of circular muscle	diameter of alimentary canal round food bolus
A	contracted in front of food bolus	wider
B	relaxed behind food bolus	narrower
C	contracted behind food bolus	wider
D	relaxed in front of food bolus	narrower

Table 3

16 The graph in Figure 8 shows the results of monitoring the heart rate of an athlete before, during and after a race over a period of 11 minutes.

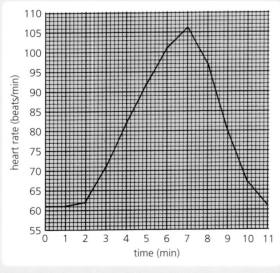

Figure 8

During which time interval (in minutes) did the greatest increase in heart rate occur?
A   2–3   B   3–4   C   4–5   D   5–6

17 Which part of Figure 9 correctly represents a pyramid of numbers?

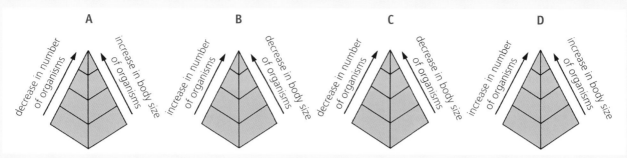

Figure 9

18 Which of the following terms means the location or spread of the members of a species in an ecosystem?

    A niche   **B** quadrat   **C** abundance   **D** distribution

19 The viral disease, myxomatosis, was deliberately introduced into Australia in the early 1950s in an attempt to control rabbit populations. Table 4 shows the results from an investigation using rabbits selected each year from wild populations and inoculated with the original disease-causing strain of the virus.

year	% population suffering fatal symptoms
1952	93
1953	95
1954	93
1955	61
1956	75
1957	54

Table 4

These results support the theory that

    A over the years an increased number of genetically resistant rabbits survived.

    B natural selection occurred between 1955 and 1957 with a peak in 1956.

    C the virus which caused myxomatosis underwent a mutation each year.

    D rabbits acquired an immunity to the disease in 1956 only.

20 The graph in Figure 10 shows the effect of increasing concentration of nitrate fertiliser on the yield of a type of crop.

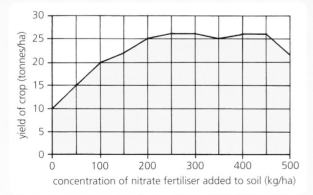

Figure 10

What is the minimum concentration (in kg/ha) of nitrate fertiliser that must be added to the soil to achieve a maximum yield of the crop?

    A 200   **B** 250   **C** 350   **D** 450

Specimen Examination 3

Choose the ONE correct answer to each of the following multiple choice questions.

1   Which row in Table 1 identifies characteristics typical of a bacterial cell?

	plasmid	cell wall	nucleus	cell membrane	central vacuole	circular chromosome
A	✘	✔	✔	✔	✔	✘
B	✔	✔	✘	✔	✘	✔
C	✘	✘	✔	✔	✘	✘
D	✔	✘	✔	✘	✔	✔

Table 1

   (✔ = present, ✘ = absent)

2   Figure 1 shows four red onion cells immersed in four different solutions P, Q, R and S.

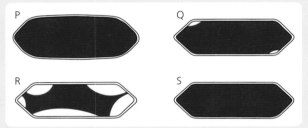

Figure 1

If the bathing solutions were arranged in order of increasing water concentration, the sequence would be
A   R, Q, S, P   B   R, S, Q, P   C   P, Q, S, R   D   P, S, Q, R

3   Which row in Table 2 correctly identifies structures 1, 2 and 3 in Figure 2?

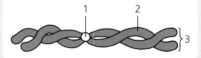

Figure 2

	1	2	3
A	centromere	chromosome	chromatid
B	chromatid	centromere	chromosome
C	centromere	chromatid	chromosome
D	chromosome	chromatid	centromere

Table 2

4   Table 3 shows the results of culturing a population of bacteria from a single cell in a fermenter for 3 hours.
    Under ideal conditions the number doubles every half hour.

time (h)	number of bacteria
0.0	1
0.5	2
1.0	4
1.5	8
2.0	16
2.5	32
3.0	64

Table 3

By how many times would the number of bacteria present at hour 3 have increased by hour 5?

A   16   B   256   C   960   D   1024

5   The graph in Figure 3 shows the effect of pH on the activity of three enzymes X, Y and Z.

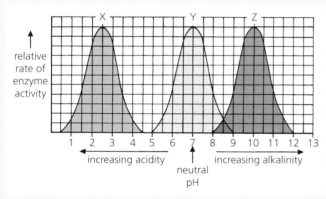

Figure 3

Which of the following conclusions CANNOT be drawn from the graph?

A   The breadth of the working range of pH of each of the enzymes is equal.
B   Two of the enzymes can be found working in alkaline conditions.
C   The region of pH scale at which each enzyme shows maximum activity is similar.
D   The optimum pH value for each enzyme differs significantly from that of the others.

6   Which of the following equations represents the aerobic breakdown of one molecule of glucose?

A   oxygen + glucose + 38 ADP + 38 P_i → carbon dioxide + water + 38 ATP
B   glucose + oxygen + 38 ATP → water + carbon dioxide + 38 ADP + 38 P_i
C   carbon dioxide + glucose + 38 ATP → water + oxygen + 38 ADP + 38P_i
D   glucose + carbon dioxide + 38 ADP + 38 P_i → oxygen + water + 38 ATP

7 The graphs in Figure 4 show the effects of several factors on the rate of photosynthesis by a green plant.

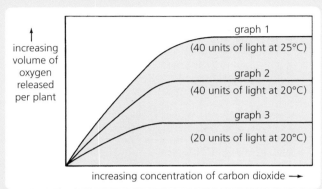

Figure 4

Which factor became limiting and caused graph 2 to level off?
A   temperature
B   light intensity
C   volume of oxygen
D   carbon dioxide concentration

8 Which of the following medical procedures does NOT involve the use of stem cells?
A   skin graft
B   cornea repair
C   hip replacement
D   bone marrow transplantation

9 The following list gives five stages that occur during a reflex action.
1   nerve impulse transmitted through sensory neuron
2   response made by an effector
3   nerve impulse transmitted through relay neuron
4   nerve impulse transmitted through motor neuron
5   stimulus detected by sensory receptor
Which of the following is the correct sequence of events?
A   1, 5, 3, 2, 4   B   5, 1, 3, 4, 2   C   1, 5, 4, 3, 2   D   5, 1, 3, 2, 4

10 Figure 5 shows part of a flower.

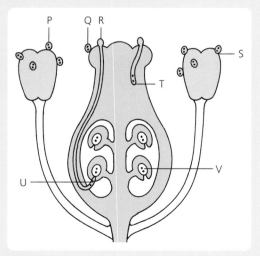

Figure 5

Which row in Table 4 is correct?

	route that represents pollination	possible site of fertilisation
A	P to Q	U
B	R to U	S
C	R to U	T
D	P to Q	V

Table 4

11 Which of the following is an example of discrete variation?
   A mass of seeds in sunflower plants
   B diameter of roots in carrot plants
   C length of seeds in bean plants
   D colour of flowers in pea plants

12 The graph in Figure 6 shows the rate of water loss from a well-watered leafy plant during a 24-hour period in summer. Which letter represents the time at which the stomata were fully closed?

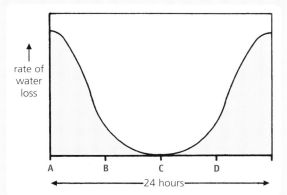

Figure 6

13 Figure 7 shows the human circulatory system. Which letter indicates the pulmonary artery?

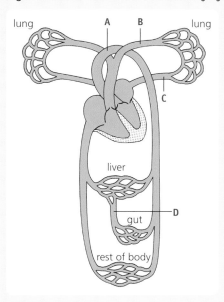

Figure 7

14 Which of the following refers to a population of organisms?
   A   all of the reptiles in a desert
   B   all of the mammals in a jungle
   C   all of the hermit crabs in a rock pool
   D   all of the flowering plants in a woodland

15 The energy content for the members of a grassland community was calculated as shown in Table 5.

type of organism	energy equivalent (kJ/m²/year)
producers	5500.0
primary consumers	330.1
secondary consumers	40.0
tertiary consumers	3.8

Table 5

9.5% of available energy was transferred from
   A   sunlight to producers.
   B   producers to primary consumers.
   C   primary consumers to secondary consumers.
   D   secondary consumers to tertiary consumers.

16 Six boxes were set up to investigate a soil food web as shown in Figure 8.

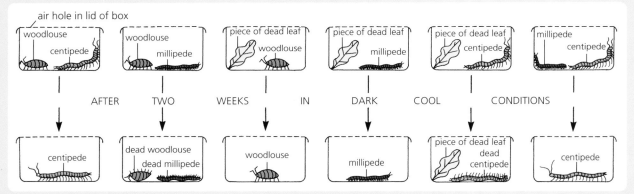

Figure 8

Which of the food webs in Figure 9 correctly represents the feeding relationships that exist amongst these soil organisms?

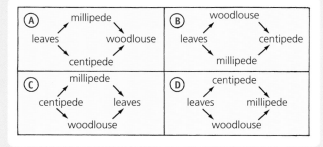

Figure 9

17 Figure 10 shows three houseplants X, Y and Z. It is followed by a key of paired statements.

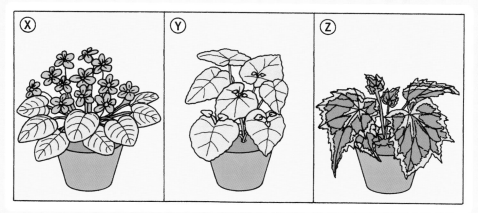

Figure 10

1 Each leaf is long and narrow in shape .... go to 2
   Each leaf is not long and narrow in shape .... go to 3
2 Each leaf is thin and has plantlets at the ends of runners..................... Spider plant
   Each leaf is thick and fleshy and lacks plantlets at the ends of runners..... Aloe plant
3 Each older leaf has a plantlet growing out of its central region .... Piggyback plant
   Each older leaf lacks a plantlet growing out of its central region .... go to 4
4 Older leaves have plantlets developing at their edges .... Mexican hat plant
   Older leaves lack plantlets developing at their edges .... go to 5
5 Each leaf is variegated .... Begonia rex
   Each leaf is not variegated .... African violet
   Use the key to establish which row in Table 6 correctly identifies plants X, Y and Z.

	X	Y	Z
A	Aloe plant	Spider plant	Mexican hat plant
B	African violet	Spider plant	Begonia rex
C	Aloe plant	Piggyback plant	Mexican hat plant
D	African violet	Piggyback plant	Begonia rex

Table 6

➡

18 Table 7 refers to some of Darwin's finches. How many different ecological niches are being exploited by these eight species?

   A 4   **B** 5   **C** 6   **D** 7

species	habitat			food		
	tree	cactus	ground	seeds	buds and fruit	insects
small ground finch			✔	✔		
cactus ground finch		✔	✔	✔		
large ground finch			✔	✔		
large cactus finch		✔		✔		
warbler finch	✔					✔
woodpecker finch	✔					✔
vegetarian tree finch	✔				✔	
insectivorous tree finch	✔					✔

Table 7

19 A thorough examination of the water at sample points 1–5 in the river shown in Figure 11 gave the results in Table 8. Which letter in the diagram indicates the pipe from which untreated sewage was being added to the river?

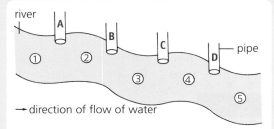

Figure 11

sample point	bacterial count	oxygen concentration	number of fish present
1	very low	very high	many
2	very high	very low	none
3	high	low	none
4	low	high	a few
5	very low	very high	many

Table 8

20 Biological control is the means by which organisms are
  A treated with antibiotics.
  B destroyed by toxic drugs.
  C killed using chemical sprays.
  D limited in number by other organisms.

Answer grid

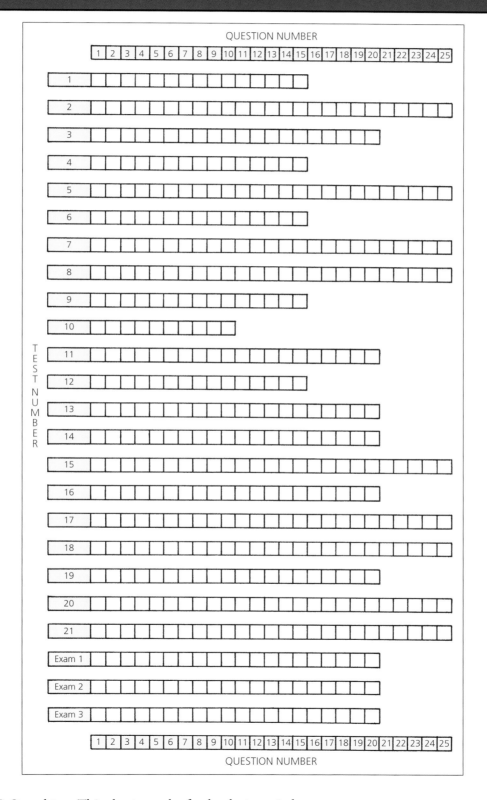

Completed answer grid

QUESTION NUMBER

	1	2	3	4	5	6	7	8	9	10	11	12	13	14	15	16	17	18	19	20	21	22	23	24	25
1	C	A	B	C	D	A	A	C	A	B	C	D	D	D	B										
2	B	C	D	D	B	A	D	D	C	A	A	C	D	B	C	C	A	B	B	B	A	B	C	A	
3	C	A	D	A	B	A	D	C	C	B	B	C	C	A	B	B	D	D	A	B					
4	D	A	C	D	B	C	A	B	C	B	D	C	D	B	A										
5	D	A	B	A	B	A	B	B	A	C	D	D	C	B	D	C	C	A	D	C	D	A	B	C	
6	B	C	C	A	A	D	C	A	B	D	A	B	D	C	B										
7	D	C	B	A	A	C	D	C	A	D	B	B	D	C	A	B	C	D	C	C	B	A	B	A	D
8	B	C	A	A	C	C	A	B	D	B	D	D	B	D	D	D	A	A	C	C	B	C	D	A	B
9	B	C	A	B	C	A	D	B	A	C	D	C	B	D	A										
10	A	C	C	B	A	B	B	D	D	A															
11	C	D	A	A	D	C	A	B	D	B	B	B	C	D	A	C	D	C	A	B					
12	B	D	B	C	A	C	B	A	B	C	B	D	A	C	C										
13	B	B	C	D	C	D	D	D	C	C	C	B	C	A	A	A	B	A	B	A					
14	A	C	B	B	C	B	C	A	B	D	C	C	A	D	A	A	D	B	D						
15	D	A	D	B	A	B	B	A	D	B	C	A	A	C	C	A	D	B	B	C	D	C	C	A	D
16	D	A	A	B	D	A	D	B	C	A	C	C	D	B	D	A	C	B	C	B					
17	D	B	C	A	A	C	A	A	D	D	D	B	A	B	A	C	D	B	C	B	C	D	B	C	B
18	C	D	D	D	B	C	D	C	B	D	A	C	A	A	B	C	A	D	A	A	C	B	B	A	B
19	C	C	C	B	B	D	D	B	D	A	D	A	C	B	C	A	A	B	A	D					
20	D	A	C	C	B	B	B	B	D	B	B	A	D	C	D	A	A	B	B	C	A	C	D	D	A	C
21	B	C	A	D	D	D	A	D	C	A	C	D	B	A	C	A	C	B	B	A	A	C	B	B	D
Exam 1	A	A	C	C	D	B	C	B	D	A	D	C	A	B	B	B	A	C	D	B	D				
Exam 2	B	D	C	D	C	A	B	D	C	A	A	C	B	D	C	B	A	D	A	B					
Exam 3	B	A	C	A	C	A	A	C	B	D	D	C	B	C	D	B	D	B	A	D					

| 1 | 2 | 3 | 4 | 5 | 6 | 7 | 8 | 9 | 10 | 11 | 12 | 13 | 14 | 15 | 16 | 17 | 18 | 19 | 20 | 21 | 22 | 23 | 24 | 25 |

QUESTION NUMBER

TEST NUMBER